Pettits Secy
Boys School.

Presented to

Bruce
Maxwell.
Vice-Captain
of School +
winner of
Prize for
Composition
July 1957.
L.G. Skinner
Headmaster

N.S.S.U., LONDON, E.C.I   PRINTED IN GREAT BRITAIN

VICE-CAPT.
COMPOSITION

THE WONDER
BOOK OF SHIPS

S.S. "PRINCE GEORGE," CANADIAN PACIFIC COAST SERVICES
Passing under Lions Gate Bridge, Vancouver.

THE " QUEEN MARY " LEAVING NEW YORK

THE WONDER BOOK

OF

SHIPS

" I must go down to the sea again, to the lonely sea and the sky,
And all I ask is a tall ship and a star to steer her by,
And the wheel's kick and the wind's song and the white sails shaking,
And a grey mist on the sea's face and a grey dawn breaking."

JOHN MASEFIELD—*Sea Fever*

WITH EIGHT COLOUR PLATES
AND NEARLY 300 ILLUSTRATIONS

SEVENTEENTH EDITION

WARD, LOCK & CO., LIMITED
LONDON AND MELBOURNE

WONDER BOOK SERIES

UNIFORM WITH THIS VOLUME

EACH WITH 8 COLOUR PLATES AND HUNDREDS OF ILLUSTRATIONS

THE WONDER BOOK OF THINGS TO DO
Provides not one solution, but many, to the perpetual question, " What can I do ? "

THE WONDER BOOK OF WOULD YOU BELIEVE IT ?
Many strange and wonderful things that are nevertheless true are described and illustrated in this fascinating volume.

THE WONDER BOOK OF DARING DEEDS
Thrilling tales of heroism and adventure on land, on sea and in the air—and true.

THE WONDER BOOK OF HOW IT'S DONE
A brightly written and lavishly illustrated volume describing numbers of the interesting things a child sees in the course of a day, telling how they work, or how they are made.

THE WONDER BOOK OF TELL ME WHY ?
Answers to numbers of those puzzling questions that begin with the words How ? When ? Why ? and What ?

THE WONDER BOOK OF DO YOU KNOW ?
Tells in picture and story of some of the most wonderful things in the world—many of them in our own homes.

THE WONDER BOOK OF ELECTRICITY
Electricity is the very wonder of wonders, and every day we find it more wonderful.

THE WONDER BOOK OF SCIENCE
Some of the most famous authorities tell the story of modern discoveries and theories.

THE WONDER BOOK OF MOTORS
Aptly described as " the Rolls-Royce " of gift books.

THE WONDER BOOK OF RAILWAYS
Scores of chatty articles about railways and locomotives all over the world.

THE WONDER BOOK OF ANIMALS
This very popular volume is not merely a picture book, or a story book, or a natural history book, but a blend of all three, with many entertaining and instructive features.

THE WONDER BOOK OF THE NAVY
All about the Navy of to-day.

THE WONDER BOOK OF THE R.A.F.
All about our glorious Air Force.

THE WONDER BOOK OF WHY AND WHAT ?
Answers to children's questions on all sorts of subjects, with hundreds of pictures.

THE WONDER BOOK OF WONDERS
The most wonderful things in the world fascinatingly described and illustrated.

THE WONDER BOOK OF NATURE
Every child is at heart a lover of Nature and the open air. Boys and girls of all ages will be delighted with this volume.

THE WONDER BOOK OF SHIPS
All about the great liners and other ships of the Merchant Navy.

THE WONDER BOOK OF SOLDIERS
A mine of information on the Army of to-day.

THE STORY WONDER BOOK
Delightful pictures and stories for boys and girls of all ages.

MADE IN ENGLAND
Printed in Great Britain by the Whitefriars Press Ltd., London and Tonbridge

THAMES SAILING BARGE

COLOUR PLATES

By courtesy of]   [*Marconi's Wireless Telegraph Co., Ltd.*

WIRELESS BEACON AERIAL AT NORTH SADDLE LIGHTHOUSE IN CHINA
The beacon sends out signals by means of which ships are able to take bearings with their direction finders

CONTENTS

CONTENTS

[*Central Press.*

FINAL TOUCHES TO THE FUNNEL OF THE CUNARD WHITE STAR
LINER " CARONIA " AT CLYDEBANK

" THE QUEEN ELIZABETH ", CUNARD WHITE STAR LINE (83,673 tons)
Sister ship to "The Queen Mary." She has two funnels instead of three and is 10 feet longer than "The Queen Mary."

THE ORIENT LINER " ORCADES " (31,000 tons)
An artist's impression.

WHERE WOULD YOU LIKE TO GO?

BRITISH STEAMSHIP LINES AND THEIR SERVICES

WHERE do all these splendid liners go ? What oceans do they voyage across, and which foreign countries do they serve ? These are the questions we naturally ask when studying the many fine vessels illustrated in this book. They will surely stir our imagination until we day-dream for a while in a world of graceful liners and the fascinating lands they visit.

Some day, we tell ourselves, we will try and make a voyage in one of those ships. Meanwhile, what better fun than to plan that voyage by trying now to decide where to go ? Because, if and when the time comes, the choice between scores of different routes and destinations will have to be made—unless you intend to become a sailor, gradually seeing more and more of the world in the course of your duties.

What is more, travelling thus in imagination only, we shall not have to wait our turn. After the toll of war there is an inevitable shortage of ships, and it will take time to replace the many that were lost in the struggle for the freedom of the seas and the world.

We shall see in the course of our voyages many strange places and races, discover time after time that the world is larger in some ways and smaller in others than we thought, and incidentally learn a

AN AERIAL VIEW OF THE "QUEEN MARY" (CUNARD WHITE STAR LINE)
PROCEEDING DOWN SOUTHAMPTON WATER

great deal of geography and commerce and of the lives and ways of the sailormen who go down to the sea in ships. It will help enormously to have at our elbows a fair-sized map, the larger the better. Perhaps you can take down the map of the world from the schoolroom wall or borrow your father's atlas.

First, you will be surprised to find what an embarrassing number of steamship lines there are from which to choose. If your map is a good one, it will probably indicate the principal services by means of dotted lines across the oceans, and you can make your arrangements with the knowledge that in normal times these services are almost as fixed and certain as the great railway routes on land.

CANADIAN PACIFIC LINER " EMPRESS OF CANADA " (20,000 tons)

An advantage of thus travelling in imagination is that when you have completed a voyage to one country by one route you can at once start by another, visiting an entirely different set of places. The Atlantic, for instance, is scored across and across, especially between England and North America. Another part of the map of the world will show routes between the west coast of America and Australia. Thus you will be able to trace a journey from England to America, then across the great continent by one of half a dozen available railways, and then by ship again to Australia and New Zealand. Or

THREE ROYAL SCOT ENGINES EMERGING FROM THE FUNNEL OF THE
" QUEEN MARY "

you can elect to make your first voyage eastward by way of the Suez Canal or round the Cape of Good Hope. In fact, the number of shipping routes indicated on the map is so great that you might think you would be in sight of shipping all day and every day. It is not until you try to estimate the distances between the ports on your voyage that you begin to realize how spacious the ocean is, and how easily ships may pass and re-pass on the same routes without sighting one another. In some parts of the map no lines are shown at all, as it is only rarely that vessels go that way.

If you are going to Australia via the Cape of Good Hope, you will learn from the map that before you leave the Atlantic Ocean you will have passed not a great distance from Ascension Island and St. Helena, which are both interesting historically, but not near enough by some hundreds of miles for you to see them. Then between the Cape and Australia you will pass, but a long distance away, the

P. & O. AND BRITISH INDIA COMPANY'S " HIMALAYA "

THE MAURETANIA (CUNARD WHITE STAR LINER)
(See page 14 for the famous old Mauretania)

"GRAND OLD LADY OF THE ATLANTIC"

The old "Mauretania" (Cunard White Star Line) has gone now, but she will never be forgotten. She held the Blue riband of the Atlantic for 20 years, and in 1929, when she was 22 years old, made her fastest crossing at an average speed of 27.22 knots. Length 790 feet, breadth 88 feet, height to top of funnels 155 feet. Quadruple screws.

THE " AQUITANIA " CONTRASTED WITH THE CAPITOL, WASHINGTON

Crozets, and the islands of St. Paul and Amsterdam, which are sometimes visited by seal-hunters and are lonely, remote places. In the last part of the voyage you will get a taste of the " Roaring Forties " and of " Running down the easting," of which you will have read in books of sea travel. Of course, no one ever really wants to be wrecked and cast on an island, but if you prefer to undergo an imaginary experience of that sort, and cannot wait until you are on your way home across the Pacific, where you may choose a coral island and a blue lagoon and coco-nuts, and all the other romantic surroundings, these inhospitable islets between South Africa and Australia will serve your purpose. Disasters at sea, however, disturb one's sailing dates, and if you have a wreck you will not be able to continue your journey.

One thing every British boy will notice with pride as he traces

THE S.S. " AMERICA ", UNITED STATES LINES

these journeys is the very large number of shipping lines leading from the British Isles. War losses would make any present comparison of tonnage misleading and valueless, but in 1939, out of a world total of some sixty-five million tons of all kinds of shipping, the British Empire owned some twenty million tons, and over seventeen million tons of this was owned in Great Britain and Ireland. Our nearest competitor was the United States of America, which, in the same year, owned about twelve and a half million tons. In America,

THE CUNARD WHITE STAR LINE M.V. " BRITANNIC "

of course, a tremendous number of ships are required for service on the Great Lakes and the long, navigable rivers of her country. Japan, Norway, Germany, Italy, France and Holland, all built very fine ships in the last few years before the war. France, for instance, had the great *Normandie* ; Italy, the *Rex* and the *Conte di Savoia* ; Germany, the *Bremen* and the *Europa*. Similar great vessels will doubtless reappear—indeed, the *Europa* is now refitting for the French as the *Liberte*. In the magnificent *Queen Elizabeth* and *Queen Mary* we possess the world's two largest liners. Splendid ships indeed, with a proud record of war service.

"THE SARPEDON" (BLUE FUNNEL LINE).

From the painting by Walter Thomas, reproduced by permission of Messrs. Alfred Holt & Co., Liverpool.

WHERE WOULD YOU LIKE TO GO?

In the middle of 1947, a notable event in North Atlantic history took place. Released from transport duties, the *Queen Elizabeth* and the *Queen Mary*—resplendent in their peace-time colours—began a regular weekly passenger service between Britain and America. In so doing, they brought to triumph a scheme first contemplated many years before; namely, that of maintaining the weekly Southampton—New York passenger service with two ships where three had formerly been required. This, rather than

[*Wide World Photos.*

THE "REX," ONE-TIME FAMOUS ITALIAN BLUE RIBAND HOLDER
ARRIVING IN NEW YORK

the incidental honour of winning the Blue Riband of the Atlantic, is what owners, designers, and builders may be justly proud of having achieved.

If your first voyage is to be to Australia, you have several routes from which to choose, and in imagination you can take them one by one in rotation. You decide to go via the Suez Canal. The Peninsular and Oriental Line (usually called the P. & O.) and the Orient Line both adopt this route, and have some of the finest and most luxurious steamers in the Australian trade. You can go aboard

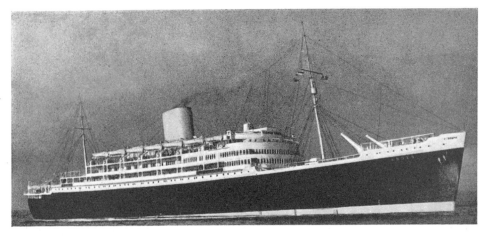

ROYAL MAIL LINES S.S. "ANDES"

at London, and in less than two days are well in the Bay of Biscay, and wondering when you will reach Gibraltar. If they wish, passengers may go overland and join the ship at a Mediterranean port. Some steamers call at Marseilles; after leaving that port you may get a glimpse of Naples, or Sicily, or Malta; then on to Alexandria and to Port Said at the entrance to the Suez Canal. You may not have time to go ashore there, but you will be interested in the crowds of natives who come alongside in their boats, if permitted, while your steamer is waiting to enter the Canal. After the Canal has been negotiated, you pass Suez and then go down the Red Sea, perhaps sighting an Arab dhow or two, with pilgrims for Jeddah, where they will land for Mecca, the Holy City of Mahommedanism; these dhows have altered little in two thousand years, and give an

ROYAL MAIL MOTOR VESSEL "CAPETOWN CASTLE," 27,000 TONS

idea of the " unchanging East." You see Aden, and if in an Aberdeen and Commonwealth Line vessel, you will call there : continuing on, you cross the Indian Ocean, either direct to Western Australia or by way of Colombo, in Ceylon. Sometimes an opportunity is afforded to go ashore at Colombo, where, if your stay is long enough, there are many wonderful things to be seen, particularly at Kandy and

SUN DECK OF THE CUNARD WHITE STAR LINER " QUEEN MARY "

in the ruined cities which the jungle is trying to swallow. If you have not time to break your journey, you will have to content yourself with watching the natives who come out in their quaint outrigger canoes to the steamer ; if the sea is rough they climb on to the outrigger to balance their frail craft. Of course they get wet, but that does not matter, for they are used to it, and their clothing consists only of a loin-cloth. Their canoes are mostly stitched together, not nailed or

WAITING FOR THE P. & O., COLOMBO
(From the painting by Dora Meeson, R.I.)

riveted. Many of the natives swim and dive like fish, and if you
throw a silver coin into the water half a dozen of them will dive after
it, and so clear is the water that you will see one of them secure the
coin before it reaches the bottom. If you throw only a copper coin
they please themselves whether they go after it or not.

The first Australian port that is reached is usually Fremantle
in Western Australia; then come, in order named, Port Adelaide,
Melbourne, Sydney, and Brisbane. If you prefer you can land at the
West Australian port and complete your journey by train, for the great
Trans-Continental railway has long been completed. If you do this
you will see something of the borderland of the great " dead heart "
of Australia, as the immense desert has been aptly called. For some
hundreds of miles the line runs straight, without anything approaching
a curve. Or you can leave the steamer at Port Adelaide and go on
by train to Melbourne, and thence to Sydney and Brisbane. It would
take too much space to mention even a few of the most interesting
sights of Australia, but you should not miss the wonderful caves at
Jenolan, which are among the largest in the world. The best of arm-
chair travelling is that when once you have voyaged to any place you

can always in imagination transport yourself there again when you have time to refer to your books and pictures.

There are other routes by which you can reach Australia. You can go by one of Messrs. Alfred Holt's fine Blue Funnel vessels or by the Shaw, Savill & Albion Company. They run a joint service known as Shaw Savill—Blue Funnel and go by way of the Cape of Good Hope, calling at Madeira, Teneriffe, Las Palmas, or Cape Town. Or, if you want to see something of the East Indies and the Great Barrier Reef off the Queensland coast—the largest coral reef in the world —you can travel by a steamer of the British India Line, which goes through the Mediterranean, the Red Sea, and the Indian Ocean, past the island of Java, and thence to the Torres Straits, where you may sight Thursday Island and its pearl fisheries, and so down the Queensland coast to Brisbane. The Barrier Reef is hundreds of miles long and several miles wide. Then, having reached Australia and seen all you can, you could take one of the fast and comfortable steamers which run from Melbourne or Sydney to New Zealand. It is strange how few British boys and girls seem to realize that New Zealand is not "just under" Australia, but considerably more than 1,000 miles away, and that the journey takes several days. In North Island you

Photo]   [E. C. Harris.

NATIVE BOYS CATCHING COINS TOSSED FROM A PASSENGER VESSEL, TORRES STRAITS will still be able to see the Maories in their homes, and in other parts of New Zealand see some of the most beautiful scenery in the Southern Hemisphere. While at Melbourne you should certainly take one of the excellent and fast coasting steamers to the island of Tasmania, and go from Launceston by train to Hobart (whose harbour some people think is as fine as that of Sydney) and indulge in a climb to the top of Mount Wellington, from which the view is superb.

If you have gone out by way of the Cape, or the Suez Canal and the Southern Australian ports, you can return to Great Britain by any of several different routes without going over much of the ground, or rather sea, you have already travelled. The return can be made via Torres Straits on a British-India liner, or by one of the steamers of the Canadian Australasian Line to Vancouver calling at Auckland, Fiji, and Honolulu on the way. Or again, by the Union Steamship Company of New Zealand, whose vessels call at all kinds of fascinating South Sea Islands on their way to San Francisco. Then there is the Shaw, Savill & Albion Company, and also the New Zealand Shipping Company, both running to London via the Panama Canal,

BLUE FUNNEL LINER "ANCHISES" LEAVING THE RIVER MERSEY

THE ROYAL MAIL LINES MOTOR VESSEL " HIGHLAND BRIGADE "

and enabling you to see one of the greatest engineering feats
of the world.   Since the Panama Canal was opened, fewer
steamers from Australia or New Zealand go through the Straits
of Magellan, and Cape Horn is left to its solitary stormy rugged-
ness except for occasional steamers.   There are other lines you
can take, such as the Blue Star Line and the Port Line, but
perhaps enough have been mentioned to show that you can travel
to Australia from Great Britain by various different routes and
companies.   Let us hope that, one of these days, you will be able
to make the voyage in more than imagination and, when " down
under," watch a Test Match played on one of Australia's splendid
grounds.

Suppose you decide to go to South America.   *En route*, you may
wish to call in at the West Indies.   If so, you can travel in one of
Elders and Fyffes' " banana " boats, which bring to Great Britain
in normal times, many millions of bananas.   You can also go on to
Central America in their ships, or you can transfer to one of the

KEY TO PLAN

SPORTS DECK.

1. Main Mast.
2-7. Ventilators.
8. Staircase.
9. Space for Sports.
10, 11. Tank Room.
12. Directional Aerials.
13. Semaphores.
14. Searchlights.
15. Chart Room.
16. Wheel-House and Bridge.
17. Officers' Quarters.

SUN DECK.

18. Verandah Grill.
19, 20. Engineers' Accommodation.
21. Cinema Projection Room.
22. Gymnasium.
23. Squash Court.
24. Lift Gear.
25. Wireless Room.
26, 28. Staterooms and Suites.
27. Staircase and Lifts.

PROMENADE DECK.

29. Cinema Projection Room.
30. Cabin Smoking Room.
31. Pantry.
32. Cabin Entrance.
33. Smoking Room.
34. Pantry.
35. After-end of Long Gallery.
36. Staircase and Lifts.
37. Ball Room.
38. Starboard Gallery.
39. Pantry.
40, 41. Lounge.
42. Chair Stowage.
43. Writing Rooms.
44. Entrance.
45. Hall and Shopping Centre.
46. Drawing Room.
47. Altar.
48. Children's Playroom.
49. Staircase and Lifts.
50. Cocktail Bar.
51. Promenade.

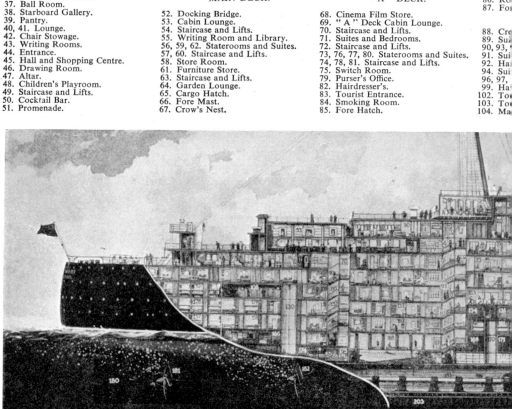

MAIN DECK.

52. Docking Bridge.
53. Cabin Lounge.
54. Staircase and Lifts.
55. Writing Room and Library.
56, 59, 62. Staterooms and Suites.
57, 60. Staircase and Lifts.
58. Store Room.
61. Furniture Store.
63. Staircase and Lifts.
64. Garden Lounge.
65. Cargo Hatch.
66. Fore Mast.
67. Crow's Nest.

"A" DECK.

68. Cinema Film Store.
69. "A" Deck Cabin Lounge.
70. Staircase and Lifts.
71. Suites and Bedrooms.
72. Staircase and Lifts.
73, 76, 77, 80. Staterooms and Suites.
74, 78, 81. Staircase and Lifts.
75. Switch Room.
79. Purser's Office.
82. Hairdresser's.
83. Tourist Entrance.
84. Smoking Room.
85. Fore Hatch.

86. Ro
87. Fo

88. Cre
89. Sui
90, 93,
91. Sui
92. Ha
94. Sui
96, 97,
99. Ha
102. To
103. To
104. Ma

THE "QUEEN

Note :—Since reconditioning " C " deck is now styled " R " deck, and "

105. Capstan Gear.
106. Crew.

"C" DECK.

107. Crew.
108. Capstan Space.
109. Bedroom Accommodation.
110, 112. Staircase and Lifts.
111. Suites and Bedrooms.
113. Cabin Dining Saloon.
114. Baker's Shop.
115-118. Kitchens, etc.
119. Bar.
120, 122. Private Dining Rooms.
121. Restaurant.

123. Foyer.
124. Tourist Dining Room.
125. Tourist Entrance.
126. Tourist Accommodation.
127. Capstan Gear and Crew's Space.

"D" DECK.

128. Crew.
129, 131, 133. Suites and Bedrooms.
130. Baggage Lift Well.
132. Cabin Staircase and Lifts.
134-144. Stores and Larders.
145. Hospital.
146. Dispensary.
147. Printers' Shop.

148, 150. Tourist Accommodation.
149. Oil-Filling Station.
151, 152. Swimming Pool.
153, 154. Tourist Kitchens.
155. Tourist Accommodation.
156- Crew.

"E" DECK.

157. Crew.
158-161. Suites and Bedrooms.
162. Tourist Accommodation.
163. Mail Discharge Room.
164. Specie Room.
165. Crew.

"F" DECK.

166. Baggage Room.
167. Bedroom Accommodation.
168. Swimming Pool.
169. Beer Stores.
170. Lift Well.
171. Wines and Minerals.
172. Garage.
173. Registered Mail.

"G" DECK.

174, 178. Baggage.
175, 176, 179. Mails.
177. Linen Store.

MACHINERY AND HOLD.

180. Rudder.
181, 182. Propeller, Starboard Side
183. Shafts and Shaft Tunnels.
184. After Engine Room.
185. Forward Engine Rooms.
186. Fan Rooms.
187. No. 5 Boiler Room.
188. Air-Conditioning Plant.
189. After Turbo-Generator Room.
190. Power Station.
191. No. 4 Boiler Room.
192. No. 3 Boiler Room
193. Forward Turbo-Generator Room.
194. Power Station.
195. No. 2 Boiler Room.
196. No. 1 Boiler Room.
197. Fan Rooms.
198. Water-Softening Machinery.
199. Tanks.
200. Baggage.
201. Mail Space.
202. Cargo.
203. Double Bottom.

[*Reproduced by courtesy of the Cunard White Star Line.*]

IN SECTION

" *decks have become* " *C*," " *D*," " *E*," *and* "*F*" *decks respectively.*

25

WHERE WOULD YOU LIKE TO GO ?

THE " CARONIA " (CUNARD WHITE STAR LINE)
(*An artist's impression*)

many steamers sailing from England to South America, some of which call in at the West Indies. You can go to Venezuelan ports with the Harrison Line, or to Brazil and the River Plate with the Royal Mail Lines Limited, visiting places like Monte Video and Buenos Aires, or again with the Blue Star Line. At some of the ports you will see something of the chilled meat trade ; for, as you know, millions of tons of beef and carcases of mutton are sent to this country. The Booth Line steamers will take you up to Manaos, a thousand miles up the River Amazon, and one of their smaller steamers occasionally goes right across Brazil into Peru—another twelve hundred miles up the Amazon. Thus, you could travel four-fifths of the way across the Continent by steamer and see something of the great forests, and perhaps catch many glimpses of the native Indians in their picturesque environments.

If you want to get direct to Demerara, in British Guiana, the Booker Line runs two steamers back and forth from there to Liverpool.

Yet another South American journey is from Liverpool to the chief ports on the east coast and as far south as Magallanes, in the Straits of Magellan, where is some of the wildest and most inhospitable scenery to be found anywhere, and perhaps up the west coast. Or you can make the journey in the other direction by going through the West Indies and the Panama Canal and down the west coast and then up the east coast. The fine liners of the Pacific Steam Navigation Company will take you to Cuba, Columbia, Equador, Peru and Chile.

On a South American trip you must not miss Rio de Janeiro, in Brazil, which large seaport has one of the most beautiful harbours in the world; indeed, some travellers think it is even finer than Sydney harbour.

The steamers of no one line touch at all the ports on both coasts, so if you want to see them all you must consult the sailings of (in addition to the companies already mentioned) the Houlder Line, the Lamport and Holt Line, the Prince Line—owned by Furness, Withy & Company, Ltd—the Donaldson Line, and the Houston Line, and also other British lines.

There are also a number of foreign-owned lines with sailings to South America, such as the Royal Holland Lloyd Line sailing from Amsterdam. The French Compagnie Generale Transatlantique has services from French ports and from Southampton to the West Indies, the Spanish Main, Colon, and to the North and South

[*Wide World Photos.*

THE " WASHINGTON," UNITED STATES LINES, OFF NEW YORK

Pacific ports ; and among others sailing from European ports are the vessels of the Scandinavian countries.

For your next arm-chair journey suppose you decide on North America. Here, again, you have a bewildering choice of lines and steamers. The Cunard White Star Line is the leading company in this most important trade ; with sailings from Liverpool and Southampton for New York and other North American ports. You might elect to travel in the giant *Queen Mary*. You will notice that on page 14 we include a picture of that world - famous Cunarder, the old *Mauretania*, the Grand Old Lady of the Atlantic. Although she has long since been broken up she will always be remembered. The new *Mauretania* is her proud and magnificent successor. There are no more luxurious ships afloat than the famous vessels of the Cunard White Star Line; they

THE " QUEEN MARY " AS SHE WOULD APPEAR IF PLACED ACROSS TRAFALGAR SQUARE, LONDON

are really travelling palaces or first-class hotels, provided with everything a passenger could desire or expect to find in a first-class hotel ashore. But you will learn more about luxury at sea in other articles.

As already mentioned, the two principal liners on the New York service are the *Queen Elizabeth* and the *Queen Mary*. Other important

WHERE WOULD YOU LIKE TO GO ?

THE FAMOUS FRENCH LINER, "NORMANDIE," 83,423 TONS
DESTROYED BY FIRE IN NEW YORK HARBOUR, 1942

ships on the North Atlantic route, some from Liverpool and some from Southampton, are the *Mauretania, Caronia, Aquitania, Media, Parthia, and Britannic*—although not all these are necessarily yet in service, After a long, grim war, ships must be reconditioned, new ones built, until gradually the whole complicated business of running great ships to schedule becomes normal again. You can sail from Glasgow by the Anchor liners, from London or Southampton by the United States Lines steamers such as the *America* and *Washington*, by British lines not mentioned, and by French, Dutch and other foreign-owned lines. Indeed, so many lines have steamers sailing for North American ports that it is possible to travel direct from nearly every important port in England, Scotland, or Wales ; these vessels are chiefly cargo steamers, but several of them carry a few passengers. When you reach the United States, a number of

CAPE HORN

railways are ready to carry you to any point on the North American continent, including San Francisco, whence you can sail for Japan, China, the East Indies, Australia, and New Zealand.

If Canada is your intended destination—which it will be when the spring comes and the St. Lawrence river is free from ice—you can choose, among other lines, between the Cunard White Star liners from London, Southampton or Liverpool, or the Canadian Pacific Steamship Company's fine Empress liners. Either of these Companies will not only take you to Canada but will book you through to any part of that great Dominion or the United States and to any port of China, Japan or Australia that it is possible to reach in connection with companies with which they have working arrange-

S.S. " VILLE DE ALGER," FRENCH LINE

ments. These companies used to send one or two of their finest steamers on what were called " yachting cruises " to Norway, the Mediterranean, the West Indies, or even right round the world.

Next, you may like a trip round Africa. You may begin with a tour in Morocco, travelling there by the MacAndrews Line from London, or Liverpool ; or by a French company, from Marseilles, which will probably include Algiers and Tunis, and enable you to go to Fez and to some of the oases in the Sahara as well, should you so desire. You will find fully a dozen lines willing to take you to Egypt. Most vessels using the Suez Canal will take passengers for the Land of the Pharaohs, and there are, further, the services of companies connected with the Ellerman and the Furness, Withy companies. To go round Africa, you can join at Port Said one of the steamers of the joint service of the Clan, Hall and Harrison Lines, starting from the Clyde or the Mersey and calling at Aden, Zanzibar and other East African ports. You transfer for the homeward journey to one of the same companies' boats which went out by the west coast and will return that way. You can take a Union-Castle steamer from London or Southampton and go by the Suez Canal and the Red Sea down the east coast, and return " round the Continent " by way of Natal and Cape Town. Having done this you can reverse the journey and go out by either of these services down the Atlantic, and return by the east coast. Another way is to land at Cape Town from one of the steamers calling there on the way to Australia, and

[*WideWorld Photos.*

THE FORMER GERMAN LINER " EUROPA," 50,000 TONS
REFITTED AS THE FRENCH LINER " LIBERTE "

return by one of the routes indicated. One of the most interesting voyages you can make from Liverpool is to the West Coast of Africa by the Elder Dempster Line. This company was the first to introduce the motor-driven passenger liner.

If you want to see all the ports in India and the Far East you will have to make several voyages, for they are served by a number of lines and no one line goes to them all, and even then you will have to change steamers to reach every one. Among the lines whose sailings you can trace are the P. & O., British India, the Ellerman Lines Limited (combining half a dozen companies), the Blue Funnel Line, the Glen Line, Ltd., the Brocklebank Line, Henderson Line,

Bibby Line, and Clan Line ; while among the foreign lines with services to the Far East may be mentioned the Danish East Asiatic Company, the Messageries Maritimes, the Nederland Royal Mail Line, the Rotterdam Lloyd Line, and the Swedish East Asiatic Company, all of which have sailings from continental ports, and other well-known lines.

You will by now have seen a great deal of the world, but there are yet the Baltic and the Mediterranean seas to visit, for either of which you will be able to arrange tours by which you can call at every port of importance, as far as the Gulf of Finland in the former, and to the Levant and Constantinople in the latter, and you will extend your journey to the Black Sea.

To finish your foreign travels you must see how many services there are between the United Kingdom and the nearer continental countries : Spain, Portugal, France, Belgium, Holland, Germany, Denmark, Norway and Sweden, and Russia too, as well as north to Iceland. You will be surprised at the number. Nor will your sea journeys be complete unless you try the trips along the British coasts ; by changing steamers occasionally it is possible to sail from Glasgow round to Aberdeen, calling at every important port and at many of the small ones in England, Wales, Scotland and Ireland.

By the time your travels are finished you should have gained some idea of the amount of this country's oversea traffic. Then probably you will want to start all over again.

Though all the names we have mentioned may seem rather confusing, if you take the trouble to look the various places out on the map and then think of all the great steamers ploughing their way to them day and night, through all sorts of weather, you will understand the force of Kipling's fine verse called " Big Steamers," and especially of the concluding lines :

> *" For the bread that you eat and the biscuits you nibble,*
> *The sweets that you suck and the joints that you carve,*
> *They are brought to you daily by all us Big Steamers,*
> *And if anyone hinders our coming you'll starve !"*

And do not forget that there are many other steamers which it has been impossible to mention in the space of this article. Remember, also, that " Tramps " are just as important to us as " Big Steamers."

A CANADIAN ICE-BREAKER

Great strength is required and the plating above and below water-line is extra thick.

H.M. TELEGRAPH SHIP "IRIS"

Specially designed and constructed for cable laying.

LAUNCH OF THE " QUEEN MARY "

BUILDING A BIG SHIP

YOU may have been puzzled by hearing people who wanted to convey an idea of the size of a vessel say " she is of so many tons." It may be as well to see what this term really means. If you put your model sailing yacht into a small bath already quite full of water, what happens ? The boat, to make room for itself, " displaces " some of the water, and this flows over the side. Exactly the same principle applies to a big ship ; the vessel and its contents weigh exactly as much as the volume of water displaced as it floats ; this is known as its " displacement tonnage." All warships are calculated on this basis, but in dealing with merchant steamships a number of other considerations have to be allowed for. It would take too long to explain in detail how the calculations are made, but they give what are known as the " gross tonnage " and the " net tonnage " of a ship. A gross ton is a hundred cubic feet of all those parts of a ship which are permanently closed in. The net tonnage, generally speaking, is the space left after allowance has been made for engine-rooms, boiler-rooms, compartments for stores, and the necessary accommodation for officers and men. As dock and harbour dues are calculated upon net tonnage, shipowners and designers take every advantage of the various deductions allowed by law, and of what are not deemed to be permanently closed-in spaces, and there is often a great difference between the gross and the net tonnage. There are, in fact, many tugs whose gross tonnage is more than a hundred and whose net tonnage, strange as it may seem, is *nil*.

When iron steamers were first introduced many people who did not understand the law of displacement contended that they must sink, and that if anything happened, such as running ashore, they would soon break up. But when it was found that iron steamers which ran ashore were less damaged by pounding on the rocks than sailing vessels which had met the like fate, confidence in the use of iron as a shipbuilding material was soon acquired.

The famous *Great Eastern*, launched in 1858, was long described as the nearest approach to an unsinkable ship that had ever been designed. If you look at the cross sectional plan of this famous vessel, which had a total length of 692 feet, you will see the arrangement of bulkheads and how a number of the features of modern liners were anticipated, notably the inner and outer " skin," or shell, the hope being that, in case of collision, only the outer skin would be pierced, and the vessel would thus still be able to float. The value of her double bottom was proved when she tore a hole about 100 feet long in the outer skin upon a rock, but continued her voyage without her safety being impaired. She was, in fact, a ship much before her

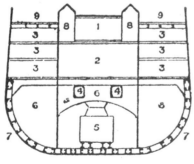

TRANSVERSE SECTION OF THE
" GREAT EASTERN "

1. Upper Saloon on Main Deck.

2. Principal Saloon in Lower Deck.

3. Side Cabins and Berths.

4. Tunnels for steam and water pipes.

6. Coal Bunkers.

7. Space between skins of ship.

8. Skylights to principal saloon.

9. Double Deck.

By courtesy of]   [Messrs. Cunard White Star, Ltd.

THE GIANT CUNARD WHITE STAR LINER, " QUEEN MARY," UNDER
CONSTRUCTION

time in size and design, and the idea of extending the double bottom well beyond the turn of the bilge (as seen by figures 7 in the sketch of a transverse section of the ship on a previous page), has since been carried still further. The old *Mauretania*, for instance, had double sides extending right round the bilge to the waterline. So it will be seen that the features introduced in that great liner launched on the Thames so many years ago have been of value, and the lessons taught by its method of construction have not been unprofitable. Sometimes it is announced that a ship is to be built on what is known

MESSRS. HARLAND & WOLFF'S DRAWING OFFICE, BELFAST
In the background is a model of a Cunard White Star Liner.

as the longitudinal system. This is a different arrangement of the ship's frame, which is claimed to give additional strength without increasing the weight of the material used. The *Great Eastern* is said to have been the first steamer in which this principle was applied, but the method of construction has since been greatly improved. All sorts of caricatures of the *Great Eastern* were published from time to time, and at last, after an eventful and not very successful career, she was broken up for old iron—although not before having laid an Atlantic cable.

BUILDING A BIG SHIP

To ensure that a ship is properly constructed and seaworthy before going to sea, she must pass the very strict examination of one of the classification societies, such as Lloyd's or British Corporation. These societies have rules, which specify the thickness and strength of every piece of metal to be used in any part of any vessel, no matter what her size. As iron is nothing like so strong as steel the latter took its place as a shipbuilding material ; the methods of producing steel have so improved that it is now as much stronger than the old sort of steel as that steel was stronger than the iron it supplanted.

By courtesy of]   [Messrs. Harland & Wolff, Ltd.

A MOULD LOFT

Consequently, to obtain the same strength as before less material is required, and this means less weight and a correspondingly greater earning power for the ship. This is not the only control exercised over the ship before she goes to sea. Another evidence of the strictness to ensure that ships are seaworthy is to be found in the free-board rules. On each side of every ship are certain marks, known as the Plimsoll marks, which show the depth to which a ship may be loaded. No vessel may go to sea which has her Plimsoll line submerged. This line is fixed in accordance with certain rules, and the vessel's free-board is the distance between the load water line, that is when she may be fully loaded, and the deck where the distance is shortest.

There is practically no limit to the size to which steamships may be built, and the only reasons why more of these immense vessels are not ordered is that they are so expensive that it would be difficult to find profitable employment for them on any route except that between Europe and New York, and that the ports they could enter are very few. The ports of Liverpool, Southampton, and New York have to be constantly dredged in order to maintain sufficient depth for large liners to enter and leave.

A ship is built on what is called the " berth," a long, slanting platform extending some hundreds of feet on shore beyond high-water line and a shorter distance into the water below. The slope is adopted so that a vessel will easily slide down when the time comes for her to be launched. The foundations of the berth have to be very firm, and may consist of thousands of tons of solid masonry or concrete. Equally necessary is the immense steel erection called a " gantry," something like the framework of a roofless shed, which has to be large enough to contain the ship from the keel to the uppermost deck. It must be many feet higher than the ship, for along the top is a double set of rails, one on each side, on which steam or electric cranes may be run, while there is often a travelling platform, also bearing rails, which extends across the gantry from one side to the other.

The preparations for constructing a ship may cost a large sum before a single plate of her keel has been placed in position. Plans to show how she is to be built must first be made ready. Steam-ships for different trades or purposes are differently shaped. Some have the engines placed near the stern ; some are to carry passengers and some are not ; other are intended to carry all sorts of general cargo ; other, again, will carry only cargo in bulk, such as grain, coal, ore, or oil. Some are to be speedy, others need not travel half so quickly. If you were going to indulge in the luxury of having a ship built for you it would be necessary first to decide what to do with her when finished so that she would prove a profitable invest-ment. This consideration determines the size of the vessel, the type of her engines, her speed, the extent and character of her passenger accommodation, and how much space is to be devoted to cargo.

BUILDING A BIG SHIP

NEARING COMPLETION—THE " QUEEN MARY "

THE " QUEEN MARY " READY FOR LAUNCHING

By courtesy of]   [Messrs. Harland & Wolff, Ltd.
ONE OF THE DECKS OF CUNARD WHITE STAR LINER " QUEEN MARY "
UNDER CONSTRUCTION

Plans have to be drawn accordingly, and then hundreds of calculations must be made to see whether the plans can be accepted or whether any improvements or alterations are necessary. Next, the builders are consulted, and they may recommend changes which experience leads them to regard as advantageous. These alterations are considered, and the effects of their adoption calculated. When all this has been accomplished for the construction of a big liner, a large wax model of the ship is prepared to scale, and in a large tank, equipped with many appliances, experiments are carried out to ascertain whether further changes are needed and whether the ship will fulfil the conditions of speed and seaworthiness expected of her. Then the plans are taken again to the draughtsmen's office and corrected and completed. The positions of all the rivets are indicated, and the sizes of the rivet-holes, to the smallest fraction of an inch, are marked on the plans. In fact, there is not a piece of steel to go into the ship which is not indicated.

Next the plans are taken to what is known as the " mould loft," where they are drawn on the floor to actual size, and all calculations as to the shapes and curves of the different parts are corrected. Before any steel parts are constructed it is necessary to make wooden patterns. Only after this has been done can a start be made with the actual building. Steel plates are riveted together to form the keel, then the frames, the deck beams, bulkheads, and other partitions, the bed for the engines, the tubes for the propeller shafts, the inner and outer shell, the upper parts of the sides, the steel decks, and so on are added, until the structure itself is complete to the bridge where the captain and his officers will control the navigation of the ship. After this she has to be launched and equipped for service.

The keel of a great vessel is put together on a wooden bed, along which are floor-plates and attachments for fastening the thick bottom frames to the keelson. These frames form, with the plating, the double bottom of the ship, and from their outer ends the side frames are built up.

By courtesy of]   [Messrs. Harland & Wolff, Ltd.
SHIPPING THE BOILERS FOR A GREAT CUNARD WHITE STAR LINER

BUILDING A BIG SHIP

When a number of frames are in position, beams are extended from side to side, to hold them together and to form the supports of the decks. The picture on page 35 shows the staging which has to be erected outside the hull during the building to enable the workmen to attach the plating to the frames. This work is continued until all the frames are in their places. The picture referred to is a striking view of the bows of the giant Cunard White Star liner, *Queen Mary*, when under construction at Clydebank. As soon as possible, the steel plates are riveted to the frames and their overlapping edges are also riveted. The turn from the bottom to the side is called the " bilge " ; and nearly all steamers have a keel built along the outside of the bilge for the greater part of their length, to lessen the tendency to roll.

When the propeller shafts and the propellers have been added, the next step is to launch the vessel. Hydraulic machinery is used to start the ship moving into the water, and the ways down which she is to slide are plentifully greased. Her movement can scarcely be felt at first, but soon the immense weight gathers speed and the ship makes an irresistible rush to the water. Launches generally take place at high tide, so that the ship shall be borne on the water as soon as possible. Heavy chains soon bring her to a standstill, and steam tugs drag the great vessel to her allotted berth for the engines and boilers to be lowered into position. Then come months in the " fitting out " basin ; in the case of the *Queen Mary*, eighteen months elapsed between her launching, and her departure from the Clyde as a completed ship.

The cabin fittings have been prepared in advance, and the change which decorators, upholsterers, painters, and electric light fitters are able to make very quickly is astonishing. Everything required has been ordered in advance, even to the smallest item, and it is said that if you show a victualling superintendent a new teaspoon he will tell you in which cupboard it is to be placed. As the size of every cabin and room is already known, all the carpets arrive ready to be put down, and every item of furniture fits to the inch into its allotted place. The pattern, too, of every decoration, of every electric fan or ventilator—for in newer vessels electric air passages, or trunks, are installed in place of the big cowl ventilators which take up so much room in the older type of steamers—and of every electric light bracket and stand is chosen beforehand. The electric power plant

CUNARD WHITE STAR LINER "CARONIA"

Final preparation in fitting out at Clydebank

on board a big liner is as effective as that of many a large town. In the *Queen Mary*, for instance, the current is supplied from the generators to no fewer than 520 separate motors, with a total horse-power of nearly 13,500. The electric lamps alone number 30,000, and the electric wires measure 4,000 miles. Nothing that can be calculated is forgotten.

Large passenger liners have their sides carried up to the bridge deck, to allow for the many decks devoted to recreation, promenading, and so on, but most vessels have one, two, or three decks only. The majority of steamers, except oil tankers, have their engines amidships.

The forepart of many steamers is raised, forming the fo'c'sle, which must not now be confused with "the fo'c'sle," or crew's quarters. At one time, sailors were almost invariably berthed forward, but this exposed them to grave danger in the event of collision and some shipowners began placing their quarters aft. Now, a law forbids the future building of ships with forward crew accommodation. Amidships is the bridge, and the deck house usually given over to the captain's and the officers' quarters; in passenger ships it is extended to form a superstructure for further accommodation. At the stern is another raised deck

By courtesy of]　　　　　[*Messrs. Wm. Denny & Sons, Ltd.*

A TRAVELLING CRANE BARGE

This useful aid to shipyard work is capable of lifting 150 tons. It is 177 feet long and is equipped with steam windlass and steering gear, electric light plant and propelling machinery sufficient to give a speed of 7½ knots.

called, according to its method of construction, a "poop" (a deck built above another deck), a raised quarter-deck, which in single-deck vessels is formed by raising a portion of the deck. The open stretch of deck between the forecastle and the bridge-deck is called the "well"; this is not covered in, because it allows any water which comes over the bows to flow away through the scuppers, and also because in its open state it adds to the safety of the vessel. Ships with a fore-well deck and an after-well deck too, are called "three island" vessels.

The average landsman generally finds it difficult to distinguish one vessel from another, but to the experienced sailor the task is comparatively easy.

Nearly all steamship companies have a distinctive house-flag of their own, and if you can distinguish this house-flag you have little difficulty in identifying the company owning the steamer. The marks on and the colour of the funnels are, however, often duplicated by several companies. By studying the peculiarities in construction of vessels you may be able to decide the period or the class to which any of them belong, but it requires a keen eye for small details to identify correctly vessels at sight.

The principal means of distinguishing vessels are the shape of the navigating bridge or chart-house, the number of decks in the super-structure, the number of funnels and their colour and position, and, in a few cases, the colour of the hulls. As, however, the great majority of steamships are painted black, little assistance is to be derived from the last.

It is easy to distinguish the cargo from the passenger boat by the smaller number of decks on the former. The average cargo steamer seldom has more than two decks, and appears to lie more deeply in the water, besides travelling more slowly. She is also usually well provided with derricks and may have "goal posts" with derricks on them for handling cargo.

There is indeed an increasing tendency for modern cargo steamers to be without masts, their place being taken by a number of derricks on posts, or on goal-post masts, as they are called when carried in pairs. The appearance of these ships is not handsome, but there is no denying their usefulness.

It is fairly easy to distinguish a Union-Castle liner, because nearly all the vessels of that Company have their hulls painted slate grey.

But so do the steamers of the Port Line, and they also have red painted funnels with black tops. Messrs. Alfred Holt's Blue Funnel Line vessels are as distinctive as any, and are recognizable anywhere.

In present-day shipbuilding, welding has in many cases superseded riveting. This means a very considerable saving in weight ; riveted plates being " overlapped " for the purpose of the riveting, whereas plates to be welded are merely laid edge to edge and " fused," or melted together by means of an electrode with a current passing through it. Thus the amount of overlapping metal in addition to the weight of the rivets is saved.

American shipyards during the war produced in vast number and with astonishing rapidity the famous "Liberty" ships, which undoubtedly played a vital part in deciding the struggle. They achieved this speedy production not only by welding the ships but by extensive prefabrication — large sections of the vessels' parts often being constructed miles from the actual building berths. Now, many modern shipyards have large spaces, or welding bays, laid out where hull parts, decks and deckhouses are assembled and welded together.

STERN VIEW OF THE "QUEEN MARY" IN KING
GEORGE V. GRAVING DOCK

THE SHIP'S OFFICERS

THE CAPTAIN, SOMETIMES!

IN the old days, before the advent of the steamship, the crew of a sailing vessel, from the captain down to the cabin boy, were virtually all sailormen—and sailormen not merely in the sense that they were following the sea as a career, but inasmuch as it was part of their everyday life to learn, and become adept at, seaman-like work. The captain and officers, having worked their way up from apprentices, were themselves practical seamen as well as navigators and disciplinarians; "Chips," the carpenter, was frequently aloft tending the spars and rigging; the sailmaker had all the sails to keep in repair; even the cook—normally in the galley, of course—was nevertheless expected to do his bit when " all hands on deck " were called to attend to this or that seamanlike job.

Science and invention have gradually altered all this. First came the early steamships, calling for engineers to look after the engines, and firemen, or stokers, to stoke their boilers; then came other developments such as wireless telegraphy, demanding trained, wireless operators; refrigerated ships, needing more specialized engineers; motor vessels and electric winches meant electricians; passenger ships demanded scores and scores of men trained in the various departments of catering for the welfare of the passengers.

So it continued until, to-day, out of a giant liner's crew of perhaps a thousand men only a proportion of them are concerned with seamanlike duties, and there may be a dozen or more other departments each playing its part in the scheme of running its " city that goes to sea."

MERCANTILE MARINE STANDARD UNIFORM

DISTINCTIONS OF RANK, ETC.

Key to Coloured Plate

In many cases the device of the Line is inserted in the diamond on sleeve

1. Certificated Master.
2.   ,,   Chief Officer.
3.   ,,   Second Officer.
4.   ,,   Third and Junior Certificated Officers.
5. Uncertificated Junior Officer.
6. Second Master.
7. First Officer.
8. Junior Second Officer.
9. Certificated Chief Engineer. All Engineer officers wear *purple* insertion.
10.   ,,   Second Engineer and Chief Refrigerating Engineer.
11.   ,,   Third Engineer and Second Refrigerating Engineer.
12.   ,,   Fourth and Junior Engineers.
13. Uncertificated Junior Engineers, Refrigerating Engineers, Boilermakers and Electricians.
14. Second Chief Engineer.
15. Junior Second Engineer.
16. Junior Third Engineer.
17. Junior Fourth Engineer.
18. Ship Surgeon. All Medical Officers wear *scarlet* insertion.
19.   ,,   ,,   Assistant.
20. Senior Purser, where three or more are carried. Pursers wear *white* insertion.
21. Purser.
22.   ,,   Assistant.
23. First Wireless Operator (sometimes *green* insertion).
24. Second Wireless Operator.
25. Third Wireless Operator.
26. Cadets or Apprentices.
27. Chief Steward on Passenger Vessels.
28. Assistant Chief Steward.
29. Steward.
30. Assistant Steward.
31. Steward on Cargo Vessels.
32. Boatswain.
33. Boatswain's Mate.
34. Quartermaster.
35. Quartermaster's Mate.
36. Cook.
37. Standard Cap Badge for Officers.
38. Peak of Master's Cap.
39. Peak of Cap for all other Officers.
40. Petty Officers' Cap Badge.
41. Mercantile Marine Coat Button.

MERCANTILE MARINE STANDARD UNIFORM

THE SHIP'S OFFICERS

Whether she is a giant liner or a more humble tramp steamer, the navigation of a ship on her voyages from port to port is the all important duty carried out by the captain and his navigating officers, who are highly trained and very capable men. The discomforts of an officer's life afloat are fewer than they used to be, but the responsibility is greater. The number of passengers carried in one ship is far higher than in the old days, and the value of the ship and cargo without counting the lives on board, has increased many times over.

Ordinary foreign-going cargo steamers carry three certificated

S.S. "MAIDAN" (BROCKLEBANK LINE)

navigating officers who rank as chief, second, and third officers, and some of the bigger ones, with their tremendous cargo holds to be looked after, carry four, as do the majority of ocean-going passenger and cargo vessels in the 10,000-ton class. The junior officer may be the fourth, or "extra third." The large passenger liners in the North Atlantic services may have as many as nine or ten, every one of whom may hold a master's certificate, and some may even have obtained their extra-master's certificate. The great Cunard White Star liner *Queen Mary*, which may be mentioned as an example to show the strength of the navigating staff employed on the splendid liners of this Company, and of the various other great lines, carries ten officers, all of whom must be men of the highest experience and hold master's or extra-master's certificates.

At the head is the captain, and then in some liners there may be a staff captain, who may be on board as the senior executive officer and be responsible for the internal discipline of the ship. The other officers follow—the chief officer, the first officer, the junior first officer, senior second and junior second, and so on. Always the captain is in supreme command, is responsible for the safety of the ship and all on board, and in a general way is expected to know everything happening. He does not keep a regular watch, but when approaching or leaving port is always on duty, on or about the bridge, and in dirty weather he will stay on duty all the time, perhaps for forty-eight hours at a stretch, for he is responsible.

In ordinary, medium-sized vessels the chief, second, and third officers take four-hour watches on the bridge in turn. The chief officer takes the 4 a.m. to 8 a.m., and the 4 p.m. to 8 p.m. watches. The second officer takes the "afternoon watch" from noon to 4 p.m., and the oft talked of "middle watch" from midnight to 4 a.m. This is generally supposed to be an unpleasant watch because it means getting up in the middle of the night, having a quick wash to banish sleepiness, and then going on duty in the dead of night and at a time when the rest of the ship is fast asleep—except, of course, the engineer officer on watch down in the engine-room and the various seamen and stokers also on the "middle watch." The third officer keeps the forenoon watch from 8 a.m. to noon, and then the 8 p.m. to midnight one.

It must not be supposed that these are their only duties. The chief officer, in addition to watch-keeping, is responsible for detailing the bosun and his seamen to the various jobs which have to be done in keeping the ship clean. On big passenger liners, the painting of deck-houses, lifeboats, and so on, is always done in dock at the end of the voyage, as otherwise there would be considerable discomfort for the passengers. But on cargo steamers making long voyages such painting is carried out by the sailors, under the chief officer's direction. Among other duties, the second officer has to care for all the ship's charts, keeping them clean and marking the course to be steered on them ; while the third officer attends to all the lifeboat gear, making sure it is in order, and looks after the ship's signal flags.

THE SHIP'S OFFICERS

In big liners, such as the *Queen Mary*, one senior and one junior officer are continually on the bridge, being relieved every four hours. The senior officer of the watch is in sole charge of the ship while on duty, unless the captain relieves him. When approaching or leaving port, however, every officer has his own special station, with its own important duties. For days before the ship sails the officers have to be on board, for there is much to do. The first and chief officers, assisted by the junior officers, are responsible for the safe and proper stowage of mails, cargo, specie, and the passengers'

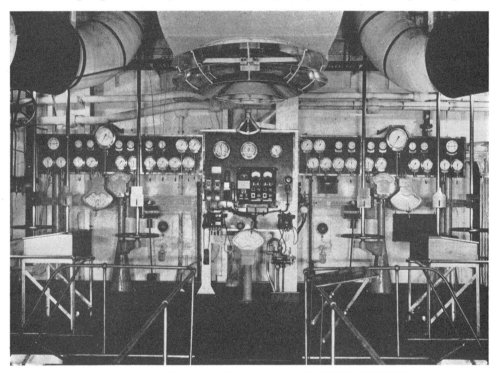

AFT STARTING PLATFORM OF THE " QUEEN MARY "

baggage which is marked, " Not wanted on voyage," and which, instead of being taken to the cabins, will go into the baggage-room. The second officer has charge of all the instruments connected with navigation. Having superintended the taking in of everything before the start of the voyage, the officers have to superintend the discharge of everything that has to be delivered at the end of the voyage, besides taking in other things for the return journey, and when they are working against time, as they almost always are when in port, they have plenty to keep them busy from early morning to late at night to get the vessel away at the scheduled hour. On all vessels, of whatever size, the captain is held responsible for every detail ; he has to satisfy himself that the vessel is properly loaded, and that the stores are on board ; but he cannot attend to everything, and many details have to be delegated to other officers. He has, however, to see personally to the formalities the Ministry of Transport insists upon before the ship can sail.

On no two vessels are the duties of the respective officers quite the same, but in general terms it may be said that the captain and the second officer are usually the navigating officers, though all the officers will take observations by the sun, moon, or stars, and compare their results with those of their superiors. In every ship the officers on duty are on the " look-out," and there are also one or two look-out men, chosen from the sailors, who stand on the forecastle head in fine weather, or in the crows' nest, when there is one, or on the bridge when high seas might wash them off the forecastle. Every officer on duty has to make note of any occurrence affecting the navigation of the ship during his watch, such as sighting wreckage, or another vessel, or exchanging signals. All important notes are entered in the ship's log, or diary, signed by the captain. Many officers make it a rule to keep a log on their own account, in which all sorts of things are recorded, and if you get a chance to read one of these unofficial logs after it has been kept systematically for a few years you will learn enough to convince you that the romance of the sea did not die out with the passing of the sailing ship. Some interesting personal experiences are given in the article " A Day in the Life of a Liner Officer " on page 205.

If you happened to be the first person to go aboard a great North Atlantic liner, and were to see the ship's company and afterwards the passengers approaching, you might be excused for wondering where they could all be put. The crew alone might number a thousand. Yet there is room in the great ship, and for more besides. You would see a dignified group of eight or ten men, in blue suits, with brass buttons and various stripes of gold braid on their sleeves, and wearing gold-braided caps ; these are the captain and the navigating officers, and immediately behind come 60 to 80 sailors. These constitute the deck department. But they would not be able to move the ship an inch if it were not for the chief engineer and his staff, though not nearly so many men are required

S. Cribb] [Southsea.

THE SEA-BOAT'S CREW COME ABOARD

53

S.S. " DE GRASSE " (FRENCH LINE) 18,435 TONS

in the engine-rooms now that oil has so largely replaced coal as fuel.

It would never do to let all these people go hungry, so 60 cooks march on board, headed by a chief cook and his specialists, whose duty it is to see that all sorts of luxuries are appetizingly set forth at every meal. The cooks, however, are too busy to serve the meals themselves, so another army of about 500 stewards comes aboard, headed by the purser and his assistants and the chief stewards of the different classes. It seems a large number of stewards, but when you make a voyage and see how much they have to do, you wonder why the numbers are not greater. Steamers in the long distance trades, like the Far East or Australia, do not have so many passengers or stewards as those in the " Atlantic ferry." On all ships some of the stewards have to attend to the dining-saloons, keeping them clean, setting the tables for meals and clearing them afterwards, and waiting on the passengers. Others are told off to look after the sleeping-cabins ; others have charge of the smoke-rooms and bars ; others, again, are deck-stewards and see that you have a deck-chair and a rug when you want them ; while yet others are in charge of the bathrooms and the gymnasium. On some steamers the gymnasium adjoins the swimming bath, and both are in charge of competent instructors ; the swimming bath, particularly, is always very popular with the younger passengers. On most liners to-day a number of stewardesses are carried to look after the lady passengers.

THE SHIP'S OFFICERS

Stewardesses' situations are much sought after; they are often given to the relatives of men who have died while in the Company's service.

Perhaps the next group to approach will puzzle you. It includes the ship's orchestra, lift attendants, wireless operators, telephone men, and the editorial and printing staffs of the daily paper published on board. The "wireless" men rank as junior officers. Every vessel with over 200 persons aboard must carry at least three operators and maintain a wireless watch "round the clock." In a big liner one operator is always on duty and often two will be kept busy all day. There are, for instance, the private messages of passengers to send or receive, the exchange of signals with passing ships to record, and the news to receive for the ship's daily paper.

But before these various companies can do their work the ship's stores have to be put into the store-rooms. Think what this means in the case of a vessel like the *Queen Mary*. Let us glance at some of the items necessary for a single voyage. The rule in all liners to-day is clean tablecloths for each meal, just as it is ashore in every first-class hotel. Thus, some twenty-one thousand tablecloths go on board, and with them a mere ninety-two thousand table napkins. In fact, taking into account the other linen requirements, such as sheets, pillow-cases, towels and the like, the colossal number of five hundred thousand pieces of linen go on board the liner. In the crockery line we have two hundred thousand pieces of earthen-

THE CANADIAN PACIFIC RAILWAY'S "EMPRESS OF FRANCE" (20,000 TONS)
Southampton—Cherbourg—Quebec—Montreal.

ware, china, and glass; while sixteen thousand pieces of cutlery and tableware are necessary.

While speaking of such impressive figures, it is interesting to note that, in the first instance, thirteen miles of fabrics were required for curtains, loose covers, upholstery, and bedspreads; and that no less than six miles of carpets and rugs were laid down in public rooms and staterooms.

Of course, except that all the linen mentioned will require laundering at the end of the voyage, and that—due to breakages—crockery replenishments will have to be made from time to time, the above items come into use on subsequent voyages. But the food that goes on board is consumed and, next voyage, a similar stock is needed. Some of the figures are quite staggering. Try to imagine your larder at home crammed full of meat. If it was a large room it might hold ten tons. The *Queen Mary's* larders have to hold seventy tons of meat, and twenty tons of fish! She needs 4,000 chickens and ducks, and 40,000 lb. of assorted vegetables; three tons of butter, and some 2,000 lb. of cheese. (Compare these amounts with the normal amount of the same items used each week in your own home.) In addition, there are thousands and thousands of eggs, and some tons of oatmeal, flour, tapioca, semolina, biscuits, and other similar foods. Think what a big shore staff is needed to get all this ready. Milk, jam, fruit, soups, tea, coffee, cocoa, chocolate, wines, spirits, mineral waters (60,000 bottles), beer, and everything else that can be thought of, whether it is in season or not, are included in the ship's stores on each voyage.

And do not forget that all these requirements must be neatly stowed away into their appointed places. To make this possible, there are, in the *Queen Mary's* elaborate kitchen system, baker's and confectioner's shops, cold larders, fruit and salad rooms, vegetable preparing rooms, butcher's and fish shops, still rooms, ice pantry, glass and china and coffee service pantries. And on what a scale, because nearly one acre of space has been devoted to the preparation and service of food.

In the first-class kitchen there are two large electric ranges, each with eight ovens for cooking the meat, and also a smaller range with ovens for the use of the cook attending to the vegetables.

An innovation on some of the newest ships is the gardener. He does not have to look after seaweed, as some might think, but after the plants and cut flowers required for table decoration at mealtimes and in the social rooms and lounges.

What is known as the "shore department" attends to the equipment, the passengers' accommodation and the food supplies, and sees that everything required for the working of the ship is sent on board. The victualling superintendent has to see that everything is supplied to the steward's department, and in this he is assisted by

A VIEW OF THE ENGINE-ROOM OF THE "QUEEN MARY"

the chief steward of the vessel, who receives reports from the different stewards under him. All the money accounts of the ship are kept by the purser's department, and as every item received on board or taken out of stores is duly checked, it will be seen that the purser and his assistants have enough to keep them busy. In the purser's department there is the ship's inspector, "master-at-arms," or policeman—there may be more than one—whose duty it is to assist in the maintenance of order. This department, in collaboration with the heads of all other departments, will allot a fire station to every member of the crew, and regular drills are carried out to ensure that, in the event of fire, everyone knows exactly what to do and there will be no confusion.

The engineering section is looked after by the chief engineer, who notifies the marine superintendent or chief shore engineer of the requirements of the engine-room, such as tools, spare parts, cotton waste and the quantity of coal or oil wanted for the voyage. The chief engineer is responsible, under the captain, for all the ship's engines. He and his assistants keep them in order and carry out whatever repairs may be necessary at sea. Some of the great liners in the North Atlantic have over thirty engineer officers, at the head of whom is the Chief Engineer, with the staff chief engineer as his immediate assistant. All big liners, in whatever trade, carry half a dozen or more engineers, and very few sea-going ships have no more than three or four. The largest liners also carry boiler-makers, plumbers, and electricians, for the engineering staff has to look after everything on board in the nature of machinery, such as steering gear, electric lighting plant, and so on, in addition to the ship's engines. Then there are the greasers for lubricating the machinery, who may number round about thirty. In the days when coal was used in large liners, it was sometimes necessary to have over three hundred firemen and coal trimmers, but to-day, in the biggest oil-burning vessels, less than a third of this number will suffice for attending the oil-fuel burners. The engineers have their regular " watches " on and off duty, night and day, for a ship's engines must be attended to all the time. Except in the smallest ships, the chief engineer does not keep a watch, but just as the captain has charge of the ship, so he has charge of the engines. When properly cared for the engines seldom go wrong, but if there be the least relaxation of care, something is sure to happen, sooner or later. You might think the engineers are standing about half the time, doing nothing. Really, they are listening to the hum and rhythm of the engines, and you would hardly believe how fond of the engines some of the men are. The engineers are such careful listeners that they can detect the smallest variation in sound as they move from one place to another, oiling a joint or connection here, or tightening a nut there. The engineers understand better than most people, what big results can spring from little causes ; the safety of the ship, her passengers, crew and cargo depends in no slight degree upon their alertness, care and skill.

Just as in the case of the previously mentioned fire stations, it is imperative that every member of the crew knows his lifeboat station, and regular lifeboat drills—at which every man must wear his lifebelt correctly— have to be carried out. Passengers, too, are required to attend these drills, and in every passenger's cabin there is a notice telling them their exact station. In a suitable foreign port, the chief officer will arrange for the lifeboats to be lowered into the water, and for the crew to be exercised in pulling and sailing.

On steamers which make long sea voyages, such as to Australia and the Far East, the proportion of provisions carried per head has to be much greater than on the big liners which take less than a week to get to New York. On most ships, moreover, large supplies

OF GREAT INTEREST TO PASSENGERS

An automatic " progress and position " indicator installed in the Royal Mail Motor Liner " Asturias." As the vessel itself progresses a little model moves correspondingly across the map. Sunrise and sunset are also represented.

of fresh water must be taken on board. Water condensed from sea water is apt to cause illness, and is therefore only used for cleaning, baths, etc.

At the end of every voyage the captain makes a formal report upon the conduct and ability of everybody employed in the ship. Every one of the crew has a discharge book, in which the captain's report is endorsed, and according to this does he stand a chance of re-employment. The captain also reports to his Company upon his officers, who must naturally set a high standard of efficiency and behaviour. The senior officers of the well-known lines are generally men who have served many years in their Company, perhaps from apprentice days, and have long since proved themselves. They are the men who look proudly forward to the time when they themselves are given command.

In some ships, so far as their duties permit, the officers associate with the saloon passengers, and sometimes have their meals in the saloon, frequently joining also in any amusements that are got up. But the modern tendency is for the officers not to associate more than is necessary with passengers. They are sometimes sadly pestered with questions.

There is a true story that a former master of a steamer in the Transatlantic trade had a speech prepared, which he used to deliver when questioning began. Taking a deep breath, he would say, without a pause, something like this:

THE GALLEY OF A LINER   [*Topical*.

"I have crossed the Atlantic 422 times I have not been shipwrecked or cast away on a desert island or been burnt at sea or marooned or shanghaied and I don't want to be The ship is doing fifteen knots and could do more if she were going faster You will be able to go ashore at New York as soon as we are alongside the jetty and not before and if you have anything you want to smuggle I don't want to know about it and I hope to retire from the sea some day. Is there anything else you would like to know?"

The concluding question would be delivered in a crescendo roar.

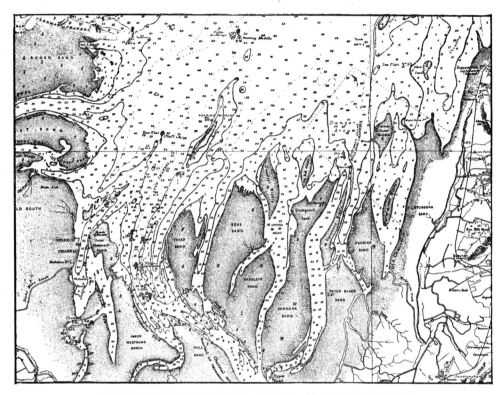

SECTION OF ADMIRALTY CHART—NORFOLK COAST

HOW CHARTS ARE MADE

WHENEVER a ship is anywhere but in dock, there is always a chart laid out on the chart-room table. This furnishes the officer on watch with all available information regarding the vicinity in which the ship happens to be. A complete set of charts needed to navigate a ship to the Far East would comprise nearly a hundred sheets. The compiling, production, and distribution of these charts is in the hands of the Hydrographic Department of the Admiralty. This is one of the most important departments and is under the direction of a Rear-Admiral. Other maritime nations have their own hydrographic services, but it can be truthfully stated that the British charts hold an unassailable position and are to be found on every ship afloat—for instance, even enemy ships captured during the war were found to have many on board. The charts are made by surveyors—naval officers who have specialized in hydrography, which is quite a profession in itself. Their naval pay is augmented by a special grant which Parliament makes towards scientific research, because, apart from its nautical value, a new survey is often of great scientific interest.

The method of making a chart depends, of course, on local conditions, but the main principles hold good in every case. The chief aim of the surveyor is to give the mariner as much information as possible concerning the depth of water and the nature of the sea bottom. This information is supplemented by details relating to the tides and currents experienced in the area surveyed. The seaman's chief professional interest in the land is the coast-line, and this is therefore delineated with great care: the heights of cliffs and hills and prominent landmarks are all used in finding a ship's position, and all are therefore ascertained with precision. A description of lighthouses and the lights they exhibit appears in all charts but those of the smallest scale.

TAKING THEODOLITE OBSERVATIONS FROM A CHURCH TOWER DURING SURVEYING OPERATIONS ON THE NORFOLK COAST

It will be seen that it is essential that every sounding, lighthouse, lightship, buoy, etc., should be marked exactly in its right position, and it is the securing of this accuracy that is the surveyor's main task and pride.

First of all the positions of all prominent marks have to be fixed relatively to each other: this is done by what is known as a triangulation, or system of triangles. Very accurate angles are measured at each prominent mark, such as church towers, etc., on the land, between all other prominent marks visible from it. Every schoolboy who has studied " trig." could calculate the distances between all the marks if he were told the distance between two of them and the angles between all the others. The photograph on this page is of a naval officer observing an angle between two conspicuous churches on the Norfolk coast from the tower of a church on the Lincolnshire coast of the Wash. The instrument he is using is called a theodolite.

When once the chief points are laid down on a chart in the making, it is an easy matter to put up small flagstaffs along the coast the position of which is fixed from the chief points. When this has been done the surveyors examine the coast-line and draw in all the details visible from seaward. Others go out in motor launches or other suitable craft to run lines of soundings with special lead and line. Accuracy is vital and great skill and patience are required as ideal conditions rarely prevail. Using a sextant and a station-pointer—both of which are instruments for observing angles—the boat's position is frequently checked by the shore marks or, when out of sight of land, by astronomical methods. (It should be mentioned, perhaps, that in big, regular surveys carried out by specially equipped surveying vessels, the latest echo-sounding apparatus and all radio aids to position-finding will also be employed.) During the progress of a survey a tide gauge is set up in a convenient position—very often on a pier—and a continuous record of the tide levels is kept. As soundings are usually " referred " to the level of low water, it is obvious that the depth of water as found by the leadsman must be corrected for the rise of tide above low water at the time the depth was measured. After every tenth sounding the lead is "armed" with tallow (that is, a piece of tallow is put in a cavity at the bottom of the lead), so that a specimen of the sea-bottom is picked up. This information is recorded on the finished chart underneath the figures showing the depths.

When all the soundings have been taken (and this is a very lengthy process, especially in countries like England, where the weather is so variable and boisterous) the work of each officer is collected and drawn on one sheet. A great deal of time is allowed for this work, as each figure is drawn with the utmost care and all the information must be marked in

PLOTTING SOUNDINGS ON A CHART

DETERMINING THE SHIP'S POSITION BY HORIZONTAL SEXTANT ANGLES

accordance with definite rules laid down by the Admiralty—for instance, there is a definite way of representing a stretch of sandy shore, or a rock which dries at low water.

The finished chart is sent to the Admiralty and may perhaps be reduced in size by a cartographer : in any case many of the soundings will be taken out, as too great a number would only confuse the mariner.

The chart is then engraved on copper plate, much of the engraver's tedious work now being assisted by an engraving machine. Subsequent necessary changes are made by beating out and re-engraving the work over an affected area. The relatively soft surface of a copper plate is protected from wear in printing by an electrolytic deposit of steel. The direct printing of charts from copper plates, however, is now to a great extent superseded by lithographic methods, the charts being printed from stones or zinc plates made by transfer from the original plates.

Each copy is carefully scrutinized, and patches of violet tinting are placed at each lighthouse. As an example of the care and forethought used by the Department it is worth mention that this paint is of such a nature as to show up equally well by artificial light as by daylight ; if it were not so, a navigator using the chart in a badly-lighted room might be misled. The charts are corrected up to the time of sale, but as new information is constantly coming to hand, the Admiralty issues *Notices to Mariners* weekly, to enable navigators to keep their charts corrected. These *Notices* are sent to all the Dominion Governments and to all the British Consuls in foreign countries, and are to be had gratis.

The Admiralty also publishes *Sailing Directions* for each ocean ; these contain much descriptive information likely to interest the navigator.

WILLIAM H. COOMBS.

8,000 H.P. MOTOR SHIP " KANIMBLA "

HOW A SHIP IS PROPELLED

ALL boys and girls, when opportunity serves, love to look at ships of all sizes ; to watch them, if in harbour, glide slowly and gracefully along, or, if at sea, roll and pitch and push their way through the waves. But how many ever pause to ask what makes a ship go forward ? What gives her the power to push through the waves, what allows her to stop when she wishes, to go backwards, and then ahead again ? Everyone watching a train can see at a glance that the locomotive, steam or electric, supplies the necessary energy, but with a ship the machinery is, in passenger-carrying vessels at any rate, hidden deep in the hull near the bottom. What is this machinery like and how does it work ?

First, you must understand that when a new ship is ordered the chances are that she will be designed for a particular service. Now, one owner may run a service of fast cargo-carrying vessels between London and, say, New Zealand, while another may own a fleet of vessels engaged in transporting coal from the Tyne to the Thames gasworks. The second owner will, in all probability, require in his ship a type of propelling machinery very different from the first. So that though many types of machinery are in use at sea, there are strong reasons for the variations, although the "father" of all types is the

By courtesy of] [*Fairfield Shipbuilding & Engineering Co., Ltd.*

MAIN ENGINES OF A BIG LINER

steam reciprocating engine, which began many years ago to be used on sailing ships as an auxiliary means of propulsion to the sails. With the historical side of the question, however, we are not concerned in this article ; our business is to talk of things as they are—a world in

STARTING PLATFORM IN THE FORWARD ENGINE-ROOM, "QUEEN MARY"

which oil is taking precedence over coal as a means of generating steam to drive turbines or reciprocating engines and in which the oil engine is operating a majority of the new tonnage laid down in world ship-yards. The oil engine is a prime mover akin to the ordinary motor-car engine except that combustion is by the heat of compression on the up-stroke rather than by spark or coil. Ships of the present day are propelled either by steam engines or by oil engines; these are the two main groups into one of which all marine engines can be placed, and each group, especially the former, can be sub-divided into two further groups—reciprocating engines and turbines.

STEAM RECIPROCATING ENGINES

What is a reciprocating engine, and why is it known by that name? Both questions will be answered in part if you look at the

THE BLADING ON THE ROTOR OR TURNING PORTION OF A TURBINE
It is against these blades that the steam impinges.

sketches on page 70. The engine consists of the following parts :— The *cylinder*, a strong tube with closed ends in which works the *piston*, a thick disc of metal, attached to one side of which is the *piston rod*, which passes through one end of the cylinder by way of a hole known as a stuffing box. This piston rod is linked by means of a joint with another round steel rod, the *connecting rod*, which in its turn is fastened by means of another joint to a *flywheel* or to a *crank shaft*. In addition, of course, there is a boiler to supply the necessary steam. That is an ordinary simple steam reciprocating engine, and it is so called because the piston itself reciprocates, or oscillates, to and fro, its motion being translated by means of the crank pin into a movement of rotation.

By courtesy of]   *[Messrs. Harland & Wolff, Ltd*

A SINGLE REDUCTION GEARED TURBINE SET, FOR MODERATE STEAM PRESSURES, WITH GEAR CASES REMOVED

On the left at back is the high-pressure turbine ; on the right is the low-pressure turbine. In the foreground is the thrust block.

Such an engine would only drive a horizontal paddle-wheel fixed to the back of a shallow-draught vessel ; it would be of no use whatever in driving a large cargo vessel. So the marine engineer has taken his simple engine and stood it on end, so that the cylinder can drive the

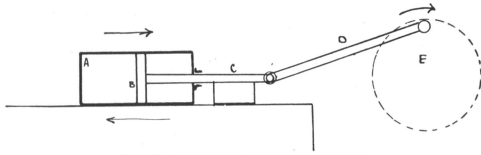

SIMPLE STEAM RECIPROCATING ENGINE

horizontal *crank shaft*, which in turn can drive the *thrust shaft*, the *tunnel shaft*, the *tail shaft*, and, finally, the propeller shaft itself: so you get an arrangement like the one in the lower sketch on this page.

How does a simple steam engine work? It all depends upon the expansive working of the gas generated when water is boiled, that is, steam. All steam-driven ships have boilers in which fresh water is boiled until it becomes steam, when it leaves the boiler through a *stop valve*, and reaches the inlet to the cylinder. Here a certain pre-determined amount is admitted, the access of more being cut off by a *slide valve*. Imprisoned by the valve, the cylinder walls and the top of the piston, what is the steam to do? It has entered at a pressure as high, in some cases, as 200 lb. per square inch. The only thing for it to do is to try to expand. In expanding it forces out the piston and, by means of the motion we have described, turns the crank shaft. Here we will leave the steam for a minute and turn our attention to the engine.

The procedure discussed has only happened on the top side of the piston, and in very early engines

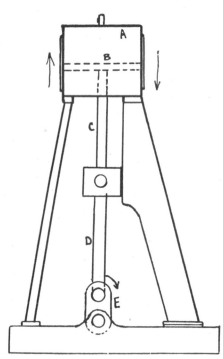

VERTICAL MARINE STEAM
RECIPROCATING ENGINE

These sketches show the essential parts of a simple reciprocating engine.

A—the cylinder.
B—the piston.
C—the piston rod.
D—the connecting rod.
E—the flywheel or crank.

70

nothing further was attempted.   However, we must have something other than the momentum of the crank shaft to push the piston back to its starting-place again, and the simplest method of returning it is to admit steam between the *under-side* of the piston, the bottom of the cylinder and the cylinder walls and let it expand and force the piston upwards again.   Such an engine is said to be *double-acting*.

This then, is how the marine steam reciprocating engine works, and it will be seen that the working depends upon the action of the slide valve

CONTROLS OF A TURBINE POWER PLANT OF ABOUT 4,000 H.P.
Note the turbines in the background.

which admits steam to one end of the cylinder, cuts it off, and then admits it to the other end of the cylinder.   The valve is really a sliding plate, alternately covering and uncovering holes in the cylinder walls, and it is worked off the crank shaft itself by means of a rod.   Since its motion must of necessity be out of phase with that of the piston, the centre of the disc working the valve rod from the crank shaft is not the point to which the rod is fixed.   The point is some distance from the centre—eccentric in fact, hence the rod is known as an *eccentric rod*.

[*Messrs. Harland & Wolff, Ltd.*

A 1,350 H.P. FIVE-CYLINDER TWO-STROKE MARINE DIESEL. A TYPE MUCH
USED IN SMALL, FAST PASSENGER MOTOR SHIPS

Now return to the steam. It must not be supposed that when
steam leaves the cylinder it has given up all its energy ; far from it.
So the engineer, in order to get the last ounce of work from his steam
and the greatest efficiency from his engine, puts the former into yet
another cylinder, of larger diameter, and repeats the expansion process.
Such an engine is known as a compound engine, having a high-
pressure cylinder and a low-pressure cylinder. You will still see
compound engines in old cargo vessels and in steam drifters or steam
launches, but most ships built within the last fifteen years or so have
triple expansion engines, in which three expansions are effected, the
cylinders being known respectively as high pressure, intermediate
pressure, and low pressure. In the days immediately before the first
use of the turbine for high speed transatlantic passenger liners
(about 1906-08) when the steam reciprocating engine was at its
zenith, this desire for extracting the last ounce of energy from the
steam was very strongly marked, and there were quadruple expansion
engines (with two different sizes of intermediate pressure cylinders) and

quadruple expansion engines with two high-pressure cylinders superimposed. Later, too, after the turbine came in, a sort of compromise was introduced between the two systems, and in ships propelled by three shafts triple expansion reciprocating engines were used on the outside shafts, exhausting into a low-pressure turbine on the centre shaft. To-day this idea has been developed even further, so that the steam drives a low-pressure turbine geared to the main shaft, thereby giving extra power without requiring more fuel consumption. Alternatively the low-pressure steam exhausts to a turbo alternator, which supplies current to a motor on the main propeller shaft. Here again, extra power is supplied without any increase in fuel consumption. In some existing ships where this has been done, hull modifications have to be made to take the extra power available.

AUXILIARY MACHINERY

What happens to the steam after it leaves the low pressure cylinder ? In a locomotive it is drawn up the funnel and lost, but in

A NOVEL METHOD OF DIESEL ENGINE DRIVE SIMILAR TO THAT EMPLOYED WITH TURBINES

Two units totalling 3,300 h.p. drive a single shaft through oil clutches and mechanical reduction gear.

73

a ship, where unlimited supplies of fresh water cannot be had for the asking, it must be used again and again, so engineers put it into what is known as a *condenser*. This is nothing more nor less than a casing containing a nest of copper pipes, over which the steam passes, and through which a stream of cold salt water is continually being poured; this cold water is sucked in and ejected by a *circulating pump*, and this is the stream of water you see pouring from a ship's side whenever her engines are working. The hot steam, coming into contact with the cold pipes, condenses, and becomes practically water again. Coupled up to the condenser is an *air pump*, which extracts the condensate, as it is called, from the bottom of the condenser and maintains a vacuum which permits the steam to rush in. After leaving the condenser, the condensate must be taken to the boiler; but as it is much better to put hot water than comparatively cold water into the boiler, the condensate is passed via the *hot well* and *hot well pump* into the *feed heater* (usually a kind of tank heated by steam) and thence by means of the *feed pumps* into the boiler again, where it is reconverted into steam.

This, then, is what makes the ship "go"; the engine, the cycle

THE PROPELLER (ONE OF FOUR) OF A TRANSATLANTIC LINER RECEIVING SKILLED ATTENTION IN DRY DOCK

HOW A SHIP IS PROPELLED

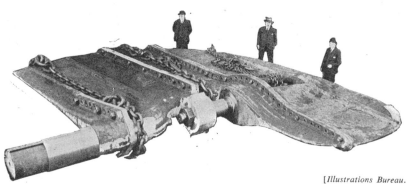

A TRANSATLANTIC MAMMOTH'S RUDDER, WEIGHING 80 TONS
This huge weight has to be operated by a steering engine.

of steam-water and water-steam operations, and the above important engine-room auxiliaries. These latter are to be found in any steam-driven ship, whether reciprocating engine or turbine—the difference is only one of prime mover, as the main propelling machinery is often called.

There is generally one condenser and one circulating pump to each prime mover. In addition there are pumps for pumping out the various tanks of the ship (bilge and ballast pumps they are called), sanitary pumps, fire pumps, and wash-deck pumps. Besides these there are *distillers* (for distilling salt water) ; *evaporators* (for evaporating salt water), and *lubricating oil pumps*, the latter being very important units in the case of turbine-driven ships.

STEAM TURBINES

Imagine a cast steel tube and inside that a smaller cylinder co-axial with the first, that is, having the same centre line. Through the outer cylinder, which is fixed to the ground, imagine little rows of vanes passing at right angles to the surface, with similar vanes projecting from the movable cylinder and fitting between the rows of vanes on the fixed cylinder. Direct steam against the fixed cylinder, or stator as we shall call it, so that the steam hits the fixed blades. It will be deflected on to the blades of the moving cylinder, or rotor, and cause this inner cylinder to revolve. This, briefly and broadly is the modern steam turbine, which is really suitable only for high-speed vessels. As in reciprocating engines, it is found advisable, in order to use all available steam energy, to compound and even triplicate turbines of high, low, and intermediate pressures, the difference, as in the case of the steam reciprocating engine, being largely a question of diameter. One of the disadvantages of the turbine is the fact that it can only run at its best at a high number of revolutions per minute—several thousand. For reasons into which we need not enter, the average mercantile propeller can only run at a low number of revolutions per minute—say 90 to 120. Hence until the advent of the *geared turbine*, the reciprocating engine had no real competitor so far as the ordinary cargo-carrying merchant ship was concerned. With the geared turbine, although the revolutions of the turbine may be several thousand per minute, by means of pinions or small toothed wheels on the turbine shafts, engaging corresponding teeth on a large wheel on the propeller shaft, the propeller shaft can be made to run at a suitable speed of 80 or 90 revolutions. In cases like this there is a high-pressure and a low-pressure turbine, steam from the former exhausting into the latter. In some modern ships a further reduction of speeds has been aimed at with a more complicated gear wheel system, known as *double reduction* gearing. A good idea of what a single reduction geared turbine set looks like with its top covers off (turbine-covers are made in halves) is given by the photograph on page 69.

OIL FUEL

Before leaving the steam side of the question, it is necessary to mention the technique of oil burnt under boilers—" liquid fuel " it is sometimes called. Oil as a fuel has many advantages ; it can be taken on board more easily and more quickly than coal ; it can be stored in parts of the ship where coal could not be placed ; it is clean ; it requires fewer men, and although more standing plant is necessary to carry out the actual burning, this fact has never proved a disadvantage. There are many different patent systems upon which oil is burnt, but the following broad method is common to most. By *transfer pumps* the oil is taken from the *bunker tanks* to *settling tanks*, whence it passes through *strainers* and *heaters*, into, in some ships, *observation tanks*, from which it is distributed through pipes to the furnace fronts at high pressure. Thence it passes to the *burners*, where it is broken up or atomized from its liquid state, finally reaching the furnace in the form of a conical spray, which ignites a few inches from the apex. Oil gives a brighter and fiercer fire than coal and enables steam to be raised more quickly and, speaking very generally, to higher pressures.

HOW A SHIP IS PROPELLED

INTERNAL COMBUSTION ENGINES

Internal combustion engines form our second great group of engines, and they are distinct in all ways from steam engines. In the steam reciprocating engine, initial energy is generated in a boiler ; in the internal combustion engine initial energy is generated in the cylinder itself by heat brought about by compression of air, which heat is sufficient to ignite a charge of refined oil, injected by means of a valve into the cylinder head. The ignition of the fuel causes an enormous increase of pressure, which can only be reduced by the driving out of the piston and the piston rod in the same way as in the steam engine. The majority of marine internal combustion

MOTOR VESSEL " IMPERIAL STAR," BLUE STAR LINE

engines, or Diesel engines, as they are generally called, are single acting, but now many vessels are fitted with double-acting internal combustion engines. Also, fuel is conveyed to the fuel valve by pressure alone and not by a charge of mechanically generated compressed air as was the case formerly. This is the difference between air and airless injection of fuel. All modern Diesels work on the latter principle, the result being compactness and a reduction of weight.

Diesel engines are built to operate either on the " four stroke cycle " or upon the " two stroke cycle." In the former there is a power impulse on one side of the piston once every two revolutions of the crank, and in the latter, by a different arrangement of valves, etc., a power impulse is given once every revolution. In the marine

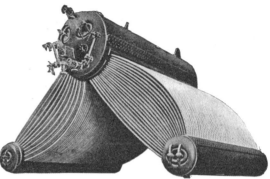

By courtesy of]   *[Messrs. J. Samuel White & Co.*

THE INSIDE AND OUTSIDE OF A MODERN OIL-FIRED WATER-TUBE BOILER

world there are many makes both of two-stroke engines and of four-stroke, but it is outside the scope of this book to list all the various kinds available. The Diesel engine requires no slide valve and mechanism, this being supplanted by valves and valve levers in the cylinder heads. Formerly there were two distinct services of compressed air in Diesel-engined ships, one of which, supplied usually by a compressor driven off a forward extension of the crank shaft, was used for injecting fuel into the cylinders at high pressure as mentioned above and the other, supplied by steam or electric-driven compressors on the engine-room floor, for starting up the engine and for manoeuvring it. The former is now almost entirely done away with. Thus it will be seen that the auxiliary machinery as well as the main machinery in a Diesel-engined ship is different from that found in a steam ship. There is, of course, no main condenser, and

By courtesy of]   *[Elder Dempster Lines, Ltd.*

MOTOR VESSEL " APAPA "

hence there are no circulating and air pumps, but there are cooling water circulating pumps for the cylinders and piston heads, to counteract the great heat generated in those parts. Then there are fuel pumps, manoeuvring compressors and lubricating oil pumps, in addition to the usual bilge, ballast, fire and wash-deck pumps. Unlike the steam reciprocating engine, there are many specialized makes of Diesel engines, all of which do the same thing in a slightly different manner. Diesel engines are now largely used for all classes of ship except certain naval vessels, while even very high-speed mercantile vessels under certain flags are motor propelled. There is another big difference between the marine steam reciprocating engine

S.S. " BEAVERGLEN," CANADIAN PACIFIC FREIGHTER (10,000 TONS)

and the marine Diesel engine. In the former the cylinders are of different diameter and the steam proceeds from one to the other ; in the latter the cylinders (usually 4, 6 or 8 in single-acting units) are of the same diameter and each is virtually an entirely separate engine linked rigidly together for purposes of strength and compactness.

Another method of propulsion sometimes adopted is known as the turbo-electric, or Diesel-electric drive. Here, the engine—instead of directly driving the propeller—is coupled to an electric generator which provides current for an electric motor situated in the vessel's stern and it is the motor which drives the propeller.

Finally, it may be mentioned that experiments are being carried out with gas driven turbines as a possible means of marine propulsion.

A. C. HARDY, B.Sc., A.M.I.Mar.E.

PART OF THE CRANK SHAFT OF M.V. " BRITANNIC " (WHITE STAR), 27,000 TONS

JOHN FITCH WITH HIS STEAMER ON THE DELAWARE, 1787

Note the curious propeller, with three threads of a screw. This type was in use for some time, until one day the propeller of a boat broke and only a single thread remained. It was then found that the boat went faster with the single thread than with three, and all future propellers were made accordingly.

THE FIRST STEAMBOATS

BOYS and girls who have read the *Wonder Book of Railways* will remember that the first locomotive, or steam-engine, as it is often called, was made by William Murdock in 1784. This was little more than a toy, however, and it was not until many clever men had thought and worked for years that the first passenger railway was opened in 1825. It ran between Stockton and Darlington, and the maker and driver of the first engine (rightly named " Locomotion ") was the famous George Stephenson.

For some time before this, however, people had been wondering whether steam-engines could not be made to drive ships along, and the story of their efforts much resembles that told in connection with the early history of railways. In the latter part of the seventeenth century a Dr. Denis Papin had made an engine consisting of a steam cylinder and piston, which he suggested might work a ship's paddles. Like so many other inventors, he was only laughed at for his pains, but later it was seen that he was on the right track, for he had recognized the importance of forming a vacuum under the piston, and it is upon this principle that all piston steam-engines are worked. In 1736 an Englishman, Jonathan Hulls, planned and patented a stern-wheel tow-boat, worked by steam. A Frenchman,

H.M. Steam Ships " Rattler " and " Alert " in 1845 towing stern to stern, and testing the relative power of the screw propeller and the paddle wheel. The " Rattler," with screw propeller, towed the paddle steamer " Alert " stern foremost at the rate of just over 2 miles per hour.   Both ships were 200 horse-power.

the Marquis de Jouffroy, in 1776, made a remarkable steamboat which had paddles shaped like the webbed feet of ducks, and in 1783 he brought out a paddle steamboat which plied on the river Saône for over a year.   It is on the Marquis's inventions that the French claim to have been the first to make use of steam-propelled vessels.

An American, John Fitch, in 1787, 1788 and 1790, made three different paddle steamboats.   The last attained a speed of about eight miles an hour.   Then Fitch went to France, where his plans were in the possession, for some months, of Robert Fulton, who later got into communication with Symington and Bell, then making experiments in Scotland.   From these three sources Fulton seems to have learned enough to enable him, in 1807, to build his famous ship, the *Clermont*.   The *Clermont* laboriously made its way from New York to Albany and back, but it was so unstable that it was necessary to lengthen and strengthen it before it could undertake a second trip, which it did in 1809.   A few days after the 1807 voyage, Robert L. Stevens, of Hoboken, New Jersey, launched the *Phœnix*, a paddle-wheel steamer, which went in a gale from New York to Philadelphia, and afterwards plied for six years as a passenger steamer on the Delaware.   Stevens's father, John, had previously experimented with a steam engine which was " the first to drive a screw propeller successfully."   His boat, built in 1804, is still preserved in the Museum of the Stevens Institute at Hoboken and a picture of it will be found on page 85. Stevens actually designed and built the hull and engines of his boat, but Fulton's engine was made for him by Boulton and Watt, in England. Thanks to his patron and supporter, Chancellor Livingston, Fulton was granted the sole right of navigating the waters of New York by steam, and Stevens's boat was not allowed to run. Fulton, therefore, was *not* the inventor of the steamboat ; all he did was to establish steamboats on the Hudson River by virtue of his monopoly. A committee of the New York State legislature a few years later decided that the steamboats built by Livingston and Fulton were in substance the invention patented by John Fitch in 1791. Fulton's *Clermont* was inferior to the *Phœnix* in every respect. It is well that these facts should be widely known, as many mis-statements are made concerning the early history of the steamboat, credit being given often where it is not due.

In Great Britain, which was destined to become the centre of the steamship-building industry of the world, William Symington, in 1789, had a small boat on the river Carron, with engines constructed by the Carron Ironworks Company. Patrick Miller, a retired Edinburgh banker, apparently paid for this vessel. In 1788 Miller himself had a man-driven, double-hulled boat on his lake at

THE " LONDON ENGINEER "
The earliest steamer between London and Margate (about 1815).

Dalswinton, and in the following year a larger boat fitted with a steam-engine ; this boat was tried on the Forth and Clyde Canal. Symington, in 1801, had a little tug, the *Charlotte Dundas*, on the same Canal ; her engine drove a wheel at the stern. Henry Bell, who had seen Symington's experiments at Carron with Miller's second boat, then designed the famous *Comet*, but it was not until July, 1812, that he was able to place his little steamer on the Clyde. She plied regularly to and fro for quite a considerable period between Glasgow and Greenock at about five miles an hour.

Other steamboats soon followed on the Clyde, and their success and comparative reliability led to their adoption on other waters. These early steamers, small as they were, were sent on voyages which we should never dream of expecting such vessels to accomplish to-day. In June, 1815, the *Elizabeth*, built in 1813, 58 feet long and of only 8 horse-power, went all the way from the Clyde to Liverpool. She was the first British steamer to undertake a sea voyage, and was in charge of a young naval lieutenant named Hargrave and his cousin, neither of whom had reached the age of nineteen. They were assisted by another boy. The *Elizabeth's* voyage was most adventurous, but the boys brought their little steamer safely through two gales and reached the Mersey none the worse for their exciting experiences. In the same year, two vessels steamed from the Clyde to London. One of these, the *Argyle* (afterwards called the *Thames*), carried two passengers from Dublin to London. When the little vessel—she was only 65 feet long and of 70 tons register—put in at Portsmouth, an Admiralty court-martial that was then sitting adjourned in haste so see the wonderful sight of a vessel propelled by steam. She was afterwards employed in the service between London and Margate.

Soon steamers were running regularly between Greenock and Belfast, and between Holyhead and Howth, near Dublin. The cross-Channel service between Dover and Calais was established immediately afterwards. But except for a few vessels built for river purposes, the steamers of that period continued to rely principally on sails, partly because the captains had always been accustomed to sails, and partly because the furnaces consumed a great deal of fuel, and space was limited. Except in entering or leaving harbour, or proceeding up or down a winding river, or when steaming against the wind, the engine was regarded merely as a help to the sails.

THE FIRST STEAMBOATS

Coastal and Continental voyages having been safely accomplished by steam, a regular service across the Atlantic was projected. The first vessel carrying a steam-engine to cross the Atlantic was the *Savannah*, a full-rigged sailing ship built at New York. She was fitted with engines and paddle-wheels, the latter being so constructed that they could be folded up and placed on deck out of the way when they were not wanted or when the weather was rough. The *Savannah* sailed from America on May 20th, 1819, arriving at Liverpool on June 20th. The voyage lasted 707 hours, and her log-book, which is still in existence, shows that her engines were used for only eighty hours, and that when she arrived at Liverpool her fuel was exhausted. As she sailed nearly all the way, it can hardly be claimed that she made the voyage as a steamer. She went on to Cronstadt, mostly under sail, and returned to New York under sail only, when her engines were removed; she remained a sailing ship until she was wrecked three years later.

JOHN STEVEN'S TWIN-SCREW STEAMER, BUILT IN 1804
Note the gear wheels.

Some years elapsed ere another steam vessel crossed the Atlantic, and in the meantime a great change had been made in the shape of the vessels, which added to their speed and seaworthiness. Practically all the steamers built in the first ten or twelve years of the industry had rounded bows, like the old wooden warships, a few of which are still to be seen doing duty as hulks. Bows of this shape are a great hindrance to speed, because of the resistance they offer to the water. David Napier noticed this, and made a voyage from Greenock to Belfast in a storm on purpose to see how the bows met the waves. He perched as far forward as he could get in order to watch the waves striking the stem and bows, and not until a big wave came and drenched him was he satisfied. He had asked the captain from time to time if he considered the sea " rough," but the captain would not admit that it was until the wave swept over the bows of the little steamer. Then he remarked that it was as rough a voyage as he remembered. " If that is all, I think I can manage," Napier replied, and went to the cabin to change into dry clothes.

The result of his observations was that he designed steamers with what are known as fine-lined or schooner bows. That is to say, his vessels, instead of having bows almost like a semicircle, had bows shaped like wedges, which easily cut through the water, and, by lessening the resistance, enabled the speed to be greatly increased without adding to the engine power. It was also found that these wedge-shaped bows rose over the waves better, and that a ship built with them would take less water on board.

The advantages of the change were so obvious that all steamers have since been constructed with wedge-shaped bows, though since the straight stem came into vogue the bows have been somewhat modified to suit the purpose for which the vessel is intended.

In 1825 two little steamers, the *Falcon*, of 176 tons, and the *Enterprise*, of 470 tons, made remarkable voyages. They went all the way to India via the Cape of Good Hope, and thus helped to inaugurate the splendid service with India and the Far East which has since developed. These two vessels had auxiliary engines and sailed most of the way. As in the case of the North Atlantic, it was some years after that regular steamship services were established.

The Canadians claim, with good reason, to have built the first steamer to cross the Atlantic. This was the *Royal William*, which must not be confused with a Liverpool steamer of the same name which was afterwards placed in the Transatlantic trade. She was built at Quebec in 1831, but her engines were made by Boulton and Watt and sent out from England. The *Royal William* crossed the Atlantic to London in 1833. She was afterwards sold to the Spaniards, who mounted some guns on her during one of the Carlist rebellions, so that she thus had the further distinction of being the first steamer on which a cannon was fired in an engagement.

THE UNION CASTLE M.V. "DUNNOTTAR CASTLE" (15,007 TONS)

THE "QUEEN MARY" ARRIVING AT NEW YORK

AN ICEBERG OFF NEWFOUNDLAND

SIGNALS AT SEA

SHIPS talk to each other or communicate with the shore in a number of ways ; in the daytime by flags, shapes, and sema-phore ; at night by lights, rockets, and flashlights, and both day and night by wireless telegraphy and telephony. The revised International Code of Signals came into force on January 1st, 1934, and if you look at the coloured plate facing page 96, you will see that in this code all the twenty-six letters of the alphabet are represented by separate flags, easily distinguishable from each other. Some flags represent not only letters, but whole messages. When leaving or approaching certain ports you may occasionally see a ship flying the A flag, the white (next the mast) and blue (with swallow tails) burgee ; this means that the vessel is on a speed trial. If possible, she should not be approached or made to slacken speed. If you see a vessel anchored apart from others in a port, or outside the break-water, and flying the red burgee B, she is loading or discharging explosives. C is the affirmative flag, meaning " Yes " ; D means " Keep clear of me—I am manœuvring with difficulty." F denotes

" I am disabled," while N flag stands for negative, or " No." P, usually called the " Blue Peter," is the most common of single flag signals, and is flown at the top of the foremast by almost every ocean-going vessel when about to leave port. It means that the vessel will sail on that particular tide, and all members of the crew must come on board. The plain yellow Q warns everyone to keep away, as the vessel may have to be placed in quarantine. Whenever a ship approaching a harbour flies this flag, she is signalled to stay outside

HOW " WINDBAG " USED TO SIGNAL HER NUMBER

until the port authorities have decided what anchorage she is to be given, and whether she is to be placed " in quarantine." If Q flies above L, it means that there is infectious disease in the ship. The flag G is the International Pilot Signal and shows that a pilot is wanted ; when he is on board, the H flag, half white and half red, is shown—usually amidships above the bridge. The signal generally used at night by a vessel needing a pilot is a " blue light," a large firework which is held in the hand and burns for about two minutes with a bright white flame. There are several other pilot signals, differing according to the nationality of the vessel using them, and if anyone should amuse himself by flying a pilot signal improperly, he is liable to a penalty of £20.

Flag signals are made with any number of flags up to four. They can relate to practically every subject under the sun ; any word or name can be spelt out and any number of figures can be given. The writer once saw a game of chess played between two sailing vessels in the middle of the South Atlantic, a mile or so apart, in which the whole of the moves were signalled by means of flags.

Many signals, especially those for an emergency, are made with two flags only, to save time, for obviously it does not take so long to hoist a signal with two flags as it would to send aloft four flags. Signals made with three flags refer to the general code and any question concerning anything whatever that a ship might want to know from another ship or from a shore signal station can be asked and answered. Cargo matters, questions of navigation, and inquiries about the weather met with on the voyage are but a few of the signals sent.

As already mentioned, it is possible to signal numbers. This is done, not with the ordinary flags representing letters of the alphabet, but with ten pennants, or long wedge shaped flags. (The Answering Pennant on the plate facing page 96 is an example of their shape.) Each one is made up of different colour combinations, and they represent the numbers 0 to 9.

The names of merchant vessels and men-of-war are indicated by a combination of four flags. If B, G or M is the topmost flag, then the vessel is British. Other countries have different flags ; P at the top is Holland. When A flag is the topmost of a four-flag-hoist, the name of some port, or headland or island is indicated.

The romance and mystery attached to flag signalling at sea are increased because the operation is picturesque and can be easily watched, though " wireless " is fast rendering it unnecessary except for vessels not equipped with apparatus and operators. It may be that a small schooner is signalling to know her exact longitude and latitude, in which case you will see some very quick work with the flags, for time is short indeed at the rate at which your steamer is travelling. Or perhaps she is announcing that she has serious illness on board, and is showing the flags MJ, " Have you a surgeon ? "

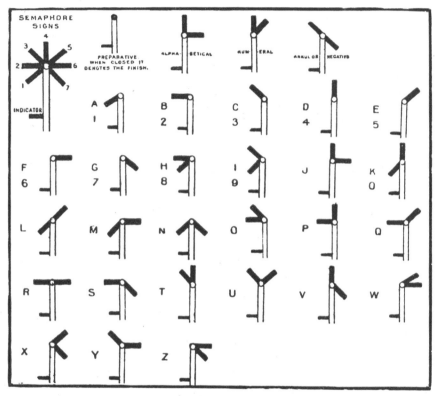

HOW THE LETTERS OF THE ALPHABET ARE INDICATED BY SEMAPHORE
The same signs, as every boy scout knows, can be made by hand flags, and read at a considerable distance.

In that case the steamer is stopped and hoists FEU, " Surgeon will come immediately." The doctor puts off with two or three men in a small boat and goes aboard to render what help he can. Probably he has risked his life half a dozen times before he reaches the ship, for ocean seas are rougher than they appear from a steamer's deck ; but in the comradeship of the sea he neither asks nor receives a fee. In many cases now it is possible to wireless all needful directions. Sometimes a vessel signals that she is short of provisions or water,

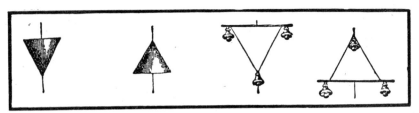

THE BAD WEATHER CONE

If the point is downwards, the gale is expected from the south; if upwards, from the north.
At night three lanterns make a triangle corresponding to the cone.

when her wants will be supplied. Or perhaps a vessel may be seen flying her national flag upside down ; it is an unofficial signal, but it is observed the world over, and indicates that the ship is in sore distress and needs immediate aid. Then, if the sea be rough, there is a call for volunteers to man the life-boat, and officers, sailors, cooks, engineers, firemen, all who can row well, in fact, come forward, and a life-boat's crew is picked.

Signalling by means of shapes has been largely discontinued, but the important distress signal consisting of a square flag with a ball or sphere above or below it, is still in use. It means, " I am in distress and require immediate assistance," and is used at greater distance, than that at which the colours of ordinary flags would be visible. Then there is the " weather " shape. This is a familiar sight at seaside resorts, and visitors easily learn to look out for the bad weather cones point upwards if the gale is expected from the northward, point downwards if the gale is looked for from the south. At night time three lanterns are used to make a triangle corresponding to the cone.

The semaphore consists of arms working somewhat like a railway signal. If only one arm is used, signalling is conducted on an adaptation of the Morse system of telegraphy, the lowering and raising of the arm corresponding to the dot and dash. Very little semaphore signalling is employed in the mercantile marine, but much of it is done by the Royal Navy.

Flag signalling by hand, usually called " flag-wagging," is more used on merchant ships than it used to be, and officers have to prove their efficiency in this, and all signals, before gaining their certificates. But as the majority of steamers now carry wireless, vessels thus equipped find this system better than any other, as it can be used when the ships are too far apart for signalling by other means.

Signalling at night by means of lights is conducted in three ways : by fixed lights, by Morse signalling lamps, and by rockets or coloured fires. Fixed lights are those which every vessel has to carry, whether under way or at anchor. From sunset to dawn every vessel—sail or steam—when under way, must show a green light on her starboard side, and a red light on her port side. These lights, which must be visible not less than two miles off, must be screened in such a way that they are not visible more than two points abaft the beam, and both must be visible directly ahead ; this arrangement is adopted so that when two vessels are approaching, each may see the direction in which the other is travelling. A masted steam vessel will carry a fixed light on her foremast, and vessels without such mast must provide some other elevated support. Steam and motor vessels carry an additional white light on their *after*masts which must be not less than fifteen feet higher than the *fore*mast light. This additional light enables their course to be more accurately determined.

A tug actually engaged in towing must carry two white lights, one above the other, on her foremast, six feet apart, and if her tow is more than a certain length, or more than one vessel, she must carry an additional light on her foremast, six feet above or below the others. Every vessel when being overtaken by another must show a light from the stern. Every vessel at anchor must show a lamp, hanging from the fore stay and another astern if longer than 150 feet. The " rules of the road " for safety at sea are based on a proper understanding of all these lights.

Flashlamps are used to signal with the ordinary Morse alphabet

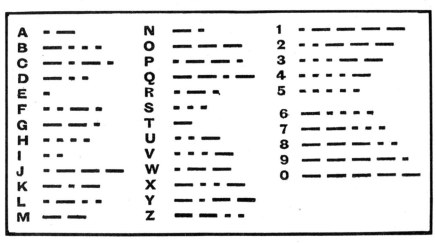

THE MORSE CODE

The short flash is of about one second duration ; the long flash of about three seconds. There should be an interval of a second between each flash or sound, or three seconds between each letter, and of six seconds between each word or group.

which is given on page 93. For daylight use there is the special Aldis signalling lamp—a modern, portable heliograph using electricity in place of the sun's rays. At night, the lamp used is generally in a fixed position above the bridge. In order to signal, the officer presses a Morse key which completes the circuit, and a " dot " or " dash " flashes out.

Rockets are used at night as signals of distress, and a continuous sounding of your steam whistle or syren has a similar meaning both day and night. Syren signals also denote alterations of course. For instance, one short blast means, " I am directing my course to starboard."

Wireless telegraphy, by which vessels communicate with one another or with shore stations over enormous distances, even across intervening land, according to the strength of their transmitting installations, has to some extent taken the place of all other forms of communication at sea. It can summon assistance if your vessel is in distress, or lead your captain to go hundreds of miles out of his course to rescue another vessel. Or it may help the meteorological office in London by supplying a report upon which the weather forecast can be based. It is the one means by which the traveller by sea can keep in touch with life ashore. A few insulated wires stretched between the masts overhead, and a " lead in " wire to the operator's cabin, are all that can be seen. But news from the outer world comes that way, and helps to fill the columns of the ship's daily newspaper.

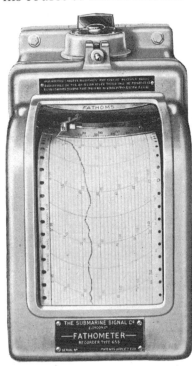

A SUBMARINE SIGNAL TO FATHOMETER

The wireless telephony call for an aeroplane in distress is " May-day " spoken three times, and then followed by the aeroplane's name or distinguishing letters and the position where she has been forced to land on the sea. Another distress signal an aeroplane may make to a ship is to circle low round the vessel and, at night, fire a succession of green Very's lights or flares. Having done this, the aeroplane should fly off in the direction of her disabled sister, in order that the ship may follow on the same course and rescue the unfortunate airmen from the water.

To-day, many vessels are fitted with complicated receiving apparatus

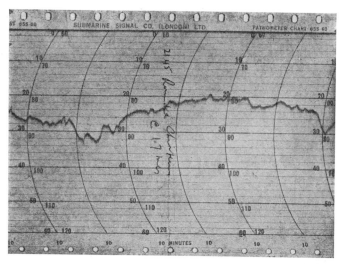

A TYPICAL FATHOMETER RECORDING

which enables them to listen for, and pick up, submarine or underwater signals sent out in fog by certain lightships, shore stations, and bell-buoys. At one time, these under-water signals were made by an electrically operated bell, but now it has been found that an oscillator—sending some form of Morse signal—is audible at a considerably greater distance, and the bell method is obsolete. The value of these submarine signals at most principal ports, headlands, and danger-points is that a ship approaching in fog can—if fitted with the necessary receiving gear—determine her position with considerable accuracy, although her captain and officers may be able to see nothing more than a blank wall of thick, swirling mist.

Radio aids to the navigator in fog are developing all the time, and in due course it may be that many older methods will be entirely superseded. For instance, there is Radar, which is described in the article on "Wireless at Sea."

Another aid to navigation in fog which may rightly be mentioned in an article on signals is the echo-sounding machine, which is an invention for finding the depth of water beneath the ship. A vessel fitted with an echo-sounding machine sends out, or signals a series of sound-waves which travel through the water to the bottom of the sea. There, they set up an echo which travels back to the ship and is received in delicate hydrophones. Special instruments measure the time taken for the echo to be heard, and record the depth.

CABIN CLASS CHILDREN'S PLAYROOM IN THE UNION CASTLE LINER
" PRETORIA CASTLE "

By courtesy of]   [The Royal Mail Lines, Ltd.

FIRST CLASS GALLEY OF A MODERN LINER
All cooking is done by electricity.

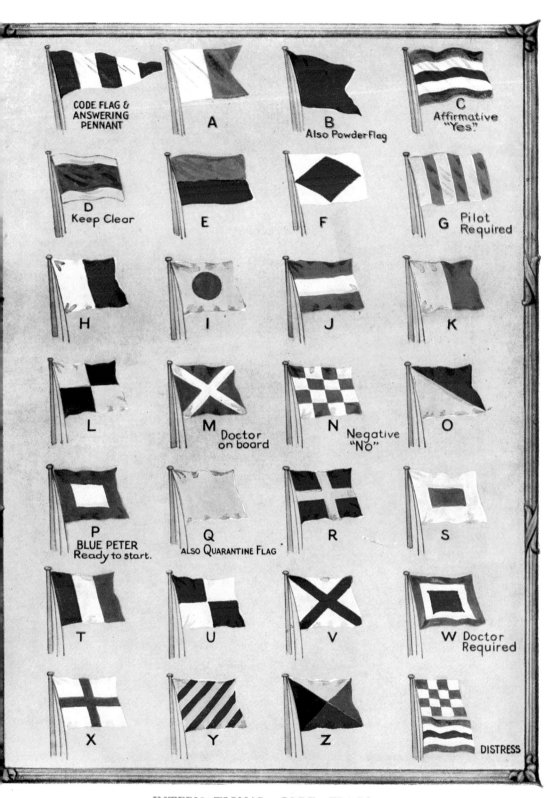

CODE FLAG &
ANSWERING
PENNANT

A

B
Also Powder Flag

C
Affirmative
"Yes"

D
Keep Clear

E

F

G Pilot
Required

H

I

J

K

L

M Doctor
on board

N Negative
"No"

O

P
BLUE PETER
Ready to start.

Q
also QUARANTINE FLAG

R

S

T

U

V

W Doctor
Required

X

Y

Z

DISTRESS

INTERNATIONAL CODE FLAGS

MEMBERS OF AN INDIAN CREW
The Serang, or chief sailor, wears a whistle on a silver chain.

OUR INDIAN SAILORS

FEW people realize the great part played by Indians, or "Lascars" as they are called by everyone except themselves, in our great shipping enterprises. Nearly every ship in the Eastern seas carries scores of them.

With the exception of a small percentage of low-caste Hindus, the Indian sailorman is a Mohammedan recruited from Calcutta, Bombay or Chittagong. The P. & O. Company usually carry "Bombay Wallahs"; the British India Steam Navigation Company favour Calcutta men; while the Clan Line Lascar almost invariably hails from Chittagong, a rising tea port in Eastern Bengal. The Asiatic Steam Navigation Company, whose activities are confined to Eastern waters, carry Laccadive Islanders, true rope and canvas mariners, who learn their trade in the quaint but daring little brigs that trade from those islands. It is a curious fact that the engine-room crews, no matter where recruited, hail from different villages from the seamen. For instance, whilst Chittagong furnishes thousands of sailors, the writer has never met a stoker from that place; these hail from Sylhet, 180 miles distant, and speak a slightly different dialect.

THE " BHANDHARY," OR SHIP'S COOK,
GRINDING CURRY ON A STONE

The saloon crews on ships where Indians are carried are very often Goanese, native Roman Catholic Christians from the Portuguese colony of Goa. Although they are essentially the same type of men, an experienced officer can recognize at a glance the part from which the Indian sailor hails. The Lascar is usually a very satisfactory seaman, clever and nimble aloft, and particularly sober and amenable to discipline, provided his officer is a man of understanding. An officer who takes the trouble to learn " Lascari," the colloquial Hindustani used on board ship, and to study their customs and prejudices, is well repaid by the extra respect given to him and the willing service rendered to the ship.

The head of a deck crew is called the " Serang," or Boatswain, and is usually assisted by two " Tindals." The Serang holds the power of a chieftain in the quarters of the crew, and his word is absolute law. It is through the Serang that the Chief Officer passes all orders for the working of the ship.

The " Quartermasters," or " Seacunnies," are of the same caste as the sailors, but generally keep much to themselves. As in all ships, they are the helmsmen, and among other duties they must keep the brass and paintwork of the bridge spotlessly clean. In port they maintain a regular day and night watch on gangway duty.

The Lascar's diet consists chiefly of rice, garnished with curries or meat, or dried or fresh fish. Their food is prepared and cooked by the " Bhandhary," or Cook, who—like his European opposite number—can, according to his culinary standard, make the crew comfortable and contented, or quite the reverse.

The Bhandhary may often be identified by a rather stooping gait, acquired through years of bending over his " curry-stone," on which he pounds the ingredients of his curries. He is almost invariably an artist with rice, which is all-important to the Lascar seaman. Indeed, it is interesting to note that before an Indian crew sign-on at the beginning of a voyage, their Bhandhary and Serang together examine samples of the rice with which their ship will be stored. There are many different types and qualities of rice, and sailors from one locality may scorn a variety which is delectable to men from another district.

With regard to his meat the Lascar insists, of course, that it be killed in the orthodox manner—freshly killed by one of his own caste.

Another interesting member of an Indian crew is generally the " Cassaub," or lamp-trimmer and store-keeper. He is usually a grizzly old veteran of the sea, who spends most of his time sitting outside his store locker, rebuking young Lascars who have the audacity to approach him for " stores."

A ship carrying a native crew as a rule has a Chinese carpenter, who is held in great respect and awe by them, and is invariably addressed as " Sahib."

The Lascar's pay is usually about £9 a month, which, though small by Western standards, makes him quite a man of substance in his own village, where he may own perhaps three wives and many cattle.

In former times, a new sailor had to pay his footing by giving part of his salary to the Serang, but this practice has ceased and crews are now engaged before a shipping master as in England.

When in a foreign port the Lascars usually go ashore in parties of four to six, wondrously clad, and always strolling in Indian file. The second-hand clothes markets of seaport towns hold an irresistible appeal for him— it is there that he can indulge in his favourite pastime of bargaining, the very spice of life to an Oriental.

One member of the crew is chosen by his shipmates to take charge of the " Koran," or native Bible. The Indian sailor is most punctilious in the observance of his religious ceremonies, and

"TOPAS," OR SWEEPER

visitors to the great docks at London or any other European port are always interested and impressed by the sight of a group of Lascars turned towards Mecca at the hour of prayer. During the " Roja," or month of fasting—which is comparable to our Lenten period—they do not eat until the sun has set.

The Indian sailor does not forget his officers' Christmas, and the saloon table at this festive season will be decorated by a spicy cake having the most highly coloured icing—and often by other delicacies the cook's fancy has dictated. These may have an unusual taste to the junior officer, but he will soon learn that they can be very appetising !

Like his British confrere, the Indian sailor endured the hardships of modern sea warfare with courage and fortitude. In spite of mines and bombs and torpedoes he continued to serve in ships with the calm, fatalistic spirit of the East—earning and receiving many decorations. Indeed, India and Pakistan may well be proud of their sailor sons.

NATIVE LEADSMAN TAKING A
SOUNDING IN AN INDIAN RIVER

SKEGNESS LIFE-BOAT AND LAUNCHING TRACTOR

LIFE-BOATS AND LIFE-SAVING

(Photographs reproduced by courtesy of the Royal National Life-boat Institution)

ALTHOUGH there are now fewer sailing vessels to come to grief on a lee shore, which was the cause of so many being destroyed in the old days, and marine engines are much more reliable than they used to be, the need for very complete life-saving services is just as great as ever it was ; in fact, the Royal National Life-boat Institution, which controls the British service, had, in 1946, its busiest year in peace time in over 120 years' magnificent service, and its life-boats rescued 647 lives. Most civilized countries have life-boat services, and we may be proud that ours is the model for the majority.

It was not until towards the end of the eighteenth century that anything much was done in the matter of life-saving. Quite apart from deliberate wrecking in order to loot the ship, there was a general and evil superstition that any man who rescued another from drowning would himself be drowned within a year, and this caused the unnecessary sacrifice of many lives. In 1765 an ingenious Frenchman designed what would probably have been a really practical lifeboat, but it was never put into use, and it was not until twenty years later that an English coachbuilder named Lukin invented his unsink-

THE " ORIGINAL," THE FIRST LIFE-BOAT, BUILT BY GREATHEAD IN 1789

able vessel, which contained many features which are still in use. Great credit must also go to William Wouldhave and a boatbuilder named Greathead. Their first life-boat was stationed at the mouth of the Tyne, where any number of the sailing colliers were wrecked every year with terrible loss of life, and was a 30-foot boat named the *Original.*

That was only a small effort, but the Duke of Northumberland of that time began to interest himself in life-boats and did a lot of good, although it was Sir William Hillary and other public-spirited men who, in 1824, founded what is now the Royal National Life-boat Institution.

The next Duke of Northumberland was not only enthusiastic in working up the organization, but by means of cash prizes and other encouragement he secured a great improvement in the design of the life-boat, and a reduction in the number of life-boat men who sacrificed their lives in gallant attempts to save others. For many years, of course, the boats had to be rowed or sailed to the wreck and back again, so that they were of limited size, with a big sheer forward and aft, which with their air-boxes and keels made them self-righting ; if a big sea capsized them, they immediately rolled themselves right way up again. At either end were white air-boxes which gave them their very smart appearance. A broad band round the hull protected it from some of the worst damage due to hard knocks, but the boats had to be built of extraordinary strength and even so they were con-

MODEL OF THE FIRST STEAM LIFE-BOAT, BUILT IN 1889

stantly being damaged, not only through their being forced through the surf in the shallow waters in which most wrecks occur, but also through being hit by the floating wreckage—masts, spars and the like—which are always to be dreaded round a wrecked ship. A heavy spar, hit end on, would go right through the planking of the strongest-built boat. In order to reach a wreck in time to be of use, these life-boats had to be very fast sailers.

Practically the whole of the longshore population of the seaport

"THE HEIGHT OF THE STORM"
From the painting by Charles Dixon, R.I.

town or village was enrolled on the life-boat list as long as they were good seamen, as all inshore fishermen were, and physically capable of such strenuous work. When the alarm was given, there was a rush for the places, only the coxswain and second coxswain having theirs by right, and as soon as the crew was complete, the boat was off. In spite of the obvious fact that power was infinitely preferable for the work to sails or oars, steam life-boats were tried only in one or two places as they had obvious disadvantages ; two of them were the time taken to raise steam and the possibility of getting the propeller fouled in wreckage.

LIFE-BOATS AND LIFE-SAVING

The 1914-18 war made as big a difference to the life-boat service as it did to practically every other phase of the sea. For years before, there had been a tendency for the population of the small fishing centres to decrease, but this was so hastened by war that the Institution found itself faced with almost insuperable difficulties in finding sufficient men who could pull an oar in the old way. Happily the motor had been made so reliable in the meantime that it could be used for life-boats and was obviously preferable to man-power, while the adaptation of the tunnel stern, which permitted gunboats

THE RESCUE
The crew of the Dover barge "Sefoy" rescued by the Cromer motor life-boat
From the painting by Charles Dixon, R.I.

to chase Chinese pirates in rivers where there was only a few feet of water, permitted the life-boat to have her screw where it was practically immune from any risk of harm.

Against that was the fact that the motor life-boat, which had to be built just as strongly as her predecessor and had to be reliable above all things, was exceedingly expensive and generally demanded a new house and new launching equipment. Also, it was necessary to have skilled engineers who would always be responsible for the maintenance and running of the engine and who therefore had to be kept on pay and not paid only by the trip as the ordinary life-boat men.

LIFE-BOATS AND LIFE-SAVING

However, motor life-boats were obviously required and the colossal task of building them was started by the Institution shortly before the 1914-18 war. Going through that war mainly as a pulling and sailing fleet, the life-boats rescued 4,131 lives : when the last war came, they were a fleet of motor boats, and their proud record for 1939-45 is the rescue of 6,376 lives.

There are several types of boat, for before a new one is placed on a station the Institution always makes a special point of having long discussions with the most experienced local life-boat men as to just

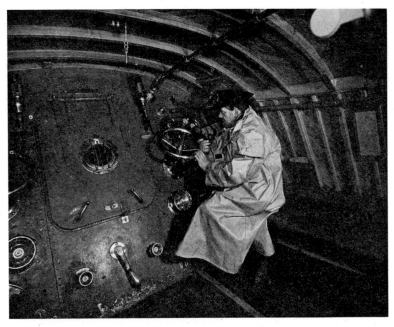

THE MOTOR MECHANIC AT HIS ENGINE CONTROLS, WITH HIS
RADIO TELEPHONE IN HIS HAND

what type would be most suitable for the conditions. A boat which would be ideal for a deep-water station, on which wrecks generally occur through ships driving on to reefs or against the cliffs, would be useless for a shallow station where the sandbanks extend for miles out to sea, raising a dangerous surf and giving very little true water in which the boat can be navigated.

The motor life-boat, with its smaller crew, permits the rescue of far more people than did the old pulling and sailing boats ; another advantage is that those with enclosed cabins afford shelter to men and women who will very likely be suffering from exposure.

"ALL SAVED"

A motor life-boat returning from a wreck.

From the painting by Charles Dixon, R.I.

LIFE-BOATS AND LIFE-SAVING

To-day, in a fleet of over one hundred and fifty life-boats, only one or two pulling and sailing ones remain. The motor life-boats are of six main types.

The biggest is the " Stromness " type, called a Barnett boat after her designer. She is 51 feet long by over 13-foot beam and with all her gear on board she weighs over twenty-six tons, so that she cannot usually be hauled up on a slipway and normally can be used only on a station where there is a harbour in which she can lie afloat at all times. She has seven watertight compartments and no less than 160 air-cases. Her crew is only eight and she can take a hundred rescued people on board. Among her fittings is a gun for throwing a line to the wreck, a searchlight and a special apparatus for spraying oil over the water ahead of the boat in order to improve the chance of rescue work.

She has twin screws, well protected, and each of them is driven by a petrol engine of 60 horse-power. The engine-room is made watertight, but in case it is flooded, as it may be through the boat being damaged, each engine is also watertight and it will go on running. The air intakes which are necessary for the engine to run, are carried as high as possible to be out of reach of the water. At full speed she can manage about nine knots and carries sufficient petrol for 180 miles " all out." Such a boat costs about £20,000 to build and equip, and about £800 per annum to maintain, provided she does not sustain too much damage on service.

The next type is the Watson cabin type, 46 feet in length, which can be launched from a slipway, although she weighs over twenty tons. She is also divided into seven watertight compartments and has 150 air-cases. Her twin engines are 40 horse-power each, her speed is rather more than eight knots, and with her crew of eight she can rescue over ninety people. With petrol engines she would be able to travel 116 miles at full speed, but most of her type now have diesel engines, which has increased their performance to 230 miles. Each of these boats costs about £18,000 and the annual upkeep is £750.

A small Watson boat, for launching off a slipway which will not take the bigger boat, is 41 feet long and weighs rather more than fifteen tons. She has eight watertight compartments and 145 air-cases ; her twin screws are driven by two engines of 35 horse-power apiece. Her speed is eight knots, she can travel 120 miles at

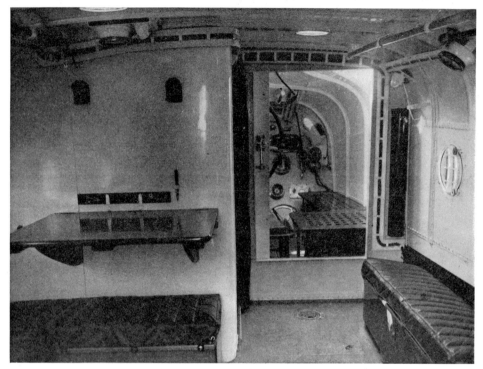

INSIDE THE CABIN OF NEW WATSON LIFE-BOAT

full speed, and she can rescue about fifty people. She cannot give the same shelter as the bigger boats, but much more than could be offered in any of the old pulling and sailing life-boats. She costs £13,500, but her annual upkeep is about the same as the 46-foot boat.

Another type, 41 feet in length and costing about the same to build and maintain, is what is known as the Aldeburgh type and is specially designed for stations, like Aldeburgh, which want a good big boat but which cannot use a harbour or slipway, so that the boat has to be light enough to be launched off the beach. The Aldeburgh type weighs just over sixteen tons, has seven watertight compartments and 135 air-cases, while her two 35 horse-power engines give her a speed of about seven and a half knots. In spite of her draught and the fact that she demands two more men than the previous types, she can rescue eighty-five people in the worst of weather.

A still lighter boat has to be sent to stations where the launching off the beach is more difficult, and for this purpose there are life-boats 35 feet 6 inches in length, costing £10,000 apiece. The two principal types are the self-righting, after the fashion of the old pulling boat, and the Liverpool type, which has greater beam. Each of these boats weighs about seven tons, has a speed of rather more than seven knots, and can rescue thirty people in bad weather.

In the next few years it is intended that all life-boats shall be equipped with two engines each and twin screws, thus obviating the need to carry sail for emergency use. It is also intended that heavy or diesel oil shall take the place of petrol, which will not only double the range of the life-boats but remove the risk of fire.

The Institution is having special all-weather wireless sets fitted, and an invention of the last war, the loud hailer, is also being put into all boats. This device enables a man's voice to be heard anything from 500-1,000 yards away instead of perhaps 50 yards away by ordinary megaphone.

It is a wonderful credit to the Life-boat Institution, and to their reputation, that the huge sums required for all this work are

THE BRIDLINGTON MOTOR LIFE-BOAT

35 ft. 6 in. self-righting type, with two 18 h.p. engines and twin screws. Note the wireless aerial.

A. H. Hawke]   [Helston.

ON THE MANACLES

forthcoming, but the heavy annual cost of maintenance and the comparatively short life of the expensive life-boats, makes the question of finance a never-ending anxiety.

The work goes on, and over 76,000 lives have been saved since the Institution was founded in 1824. But if we think of the life-boats coming gloriously and triumphantly through the storms, we must remember, also, the constant danger the life-boat men face. In the last twenty years, 56 of these brave fellows gave their lives in the saving of 12,000 people. The tragedy of the Mumbles life-boat in 1947 is surely still fresh in our memories—eight Mumbles men drowned when their life-boat capsized in a gale of exceptional severity. Yet within eight weeks this small fishing village had provided another crew—all of them Mumbles men—to man the Institution's new life-boat. That is the spirit of our Life-boat Service.

When the danger spot is close inshore, where in ordinary circumstances it would be suicide to take even the most powerful of life-boats, there are rocket stations owned and maintained by the Ministry of Transport and operated by the coastguards and volunteer helpers.

Should a ship be wrecked close inshore, the whole apparatus is designed to be so compact and light that it can be loaded on to a lorry and taken to the nearest point without a moment's delay. The gun consists of a tripod with two short legs and one long one, the latter forming the barrel. The object is to fire the rocket so that it goes over the wreck ; as may be imagined, a big allowance has to be made for the wind in the sort of storm most likely to produce a wreck. To the tail of each rocket is made fast a length of thin but very strong line somewhat like that used by whalers for their harpoons. If a good shot is made and the rocket carries over the deck of the wreck, this line will fall within reach of the men, and by it they can haul off to the ship a thick rope with a pulley and a long light line called the whip. The thick rope is made fast as high above the water as possible and with the whip the people on shore haul out a " travel-ler," to which is attached an ordinary lifebuoy with a pair of canvas breeches under it. It is not by any means a pleasant experience to be pulled through the surf in such an appliance, but it is far better than being drowned, and many lives are saved all round the coast by this apparatus.

At the same time it is admitted that it is not by any means ideal. Firstly, the distressed crew must be in a condition to help themselves, to haul in the line when it is thrown across their deck,

A. H. Hawke]　　　　　　　　　　　　　　　　　　　　　　　　　[Helston.
THE CAPTAIN OF A WRECKED SAILING SHIP BEING RESCUED BY
BREECHES-BUOY

and often enough they are quite incapable of doing that. Again, there have been many cases where the man being rescued, almost within reach of safety, has been thrown by a wave against the heavy block over his head and brained.

It is obvious that it will very often be a lee shore on which a ship will come to grief ; that is to say, one towards which the wind is blowing. The rocket apparatus on shore, therefore, has to throw its line against the full force of the gale, and one of the wisest life-saving regulations is that all ships of more than a certain size shall carry on board a gun, rocket or other apparatus capable of throwing a line. As they will do it with the wind, they have a far better chance of their line carrying far enough ; in addition to which, the land is a much easier mark to aim at than a small ship. Once communication is established, the heavy line is hauled out to the ship in the same way and the breeches-buoy hauled backwards and forwards along it.

WATSON BOAT, ST. HELIER, JERSEY
46 ft. 9 in., she is the first to have a deck cabin, and she has two 40 h.p. diesel engines.

ICELANDIC TRAWLER

THE " ROYAL SOVEREIGN "
This is one of the largest of the fleet of British lightships dotted around the coast of Great Britain.
Stationed 280°, 4 miles, 8½ cables from Beachy Head.

A FULL-RIGGED SHIP IN FULL SAIL

[Topical.

SAILING SHIPS AND THEIR RIGS:

HOW TO KNOW AND DESCRIBE THEM

THERE is romance and interest in all ships, and the romance of sail is readily understood. Those old tall ships are rapidly disappearing but their beauty will remain in the minds of lovers of ships for all time, and there are many enthusiasts who like to study the way in which they developed and were handled.

It all began with the single square sail of the very ancient ship which drove her along only when the wind was fair. When it was foul they simply dropped anchor and waited for a change. Time meant little in those days. The first development, dating back at least to Roman times, was a topsail over the original square sail. Then the scouting ships of fighting fleets, and the pirates, decided that they wanted to make progress through the water even when the wind was not right astern. This demanded a sail more in line with the

[*Nautical.*

AMERICAN SIX-MASTED SCHOONER, "WYOMING"

These large schooners were capable of crossing the Atlantic with a crew of twelve men.

keel rather than at right angles to it, and was achieved by canting the square sail and its yard at an angle. The shape of the sail gradually changed, also, until it became the lug-sail in Northern Europe and the lateen in the Mediterranean. These vessels could not sail nearly as close to the wind as the various types which later developed from them but they did very much better than their predecessors.

This fore-and-aft rig was applied only to small craft for special purposes; the bigger ships, whether merchantmen or men-of-war, remained square rigged, although—to make them handier—their sails were later combined with fore-and-aft canvas on one or more masts. As their size increased more and taller masts were fitted in order to carry the additional canvas. Thus the rig became gradually more complicated. The original square sail became the course, from the French word *corse* or body, and above that the topsail was revived from Roman days and set on a yard. Even that was insufficient, so the topgallant was set over that and, finally, the royal. In the prime days of sail there were all sorts of flying kites set above the royals—skysails, moonrakers and others but it is doubtful whether they materially increased a ship's speed.

114

SAILING SHIPS AND THEIR RIGS

Still more sail area was demanded. But, unless they were to be blown out of the ship in heavy weather, the masts could be no taller. So the sail plan was extended sideways by means of studding sails, called stu'nsails by the sailor. These were carried only in light airs when it was necessary to catch every breath of wind, and were set on stu'nsail booms lashed to the ends of the yards. They could be used only with the wind dead astern and, considering the tremendous work of setting them and taking them in again before they blew away, their value was always doubtful and their use was eventually abandoned.

As trade became more complex and merchant ships explored more remote seas, extra rigs were required to provide just the right kind of ship for this or that particular work. Some were square rigged, others fore-and-aft, while others again were a mixture of both. But every one, and every slight change, was given its own name. In ancient days the classification of sailing ships had been simple ; a big vessel was a ship, a medium-sized one was a barque, and a very small one was a pinnace—the old-time navigators being unconcerned

H. Hughes & Son, Ltd.]   [*London*
BARQUE " SERRANA " (ABOUT 1,400 TONS)

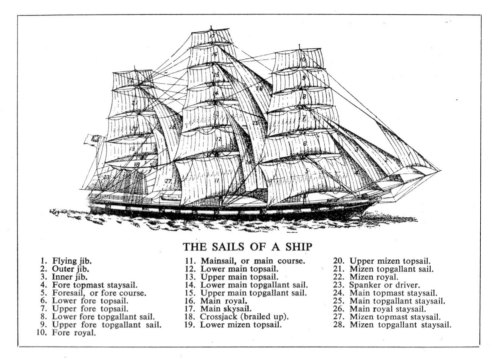

THE SAILS OF A SHIP

1. Flying jib.	11. Mainsail, or main course.	20. Upper mizen topsail.
2. Outer jib.	12. Lower main topsail.	21. Mizen topgallant sail.
3. Inner jib.	13. Upper main topsail.	22. Mizen royal.
4. Fore topmast staysail.	14. Lower main topgallant sail.	23. Spanker or driver.
5. Foresail, or fore course.	15. Upper main topgallant sail.	24. Main topmast staysail.
6. Lower fore topsail.	16. Main royal.	25. Main topgallant staysail.
7. Upper fore topsail.	17. Main skysail.	26. Main royal staysail.
8. Lower fore topgallant sail.	18. Crossjack (brailed up).	27. Mizen topmast staysail.
9. Upper fore topgallant sail.	19. Lower mizen topsail.	28. Mizen topgallant staysail.
10. Fore royal.		

with naming their vessels according to the arrangement of masts and sails. Later, however, this became a matter of very exact definition.

The name " ship " was applied only to a sailing vessel with three or more masts, square rigged on all of them. The most usual type was the three-masted ship, the rig adopted in all the fastest clipper ships ; later, there were a number of four-masters—a somewhat inconvenient rig—and one five-masted ship, the German *Preussen*, which was wrecked after a collision near Dover.

Fewer men were necessary in handling a fore-and-aft rig, which was found handier in other ways, and this led to the type of sailing vessel known as a " barque ". The name no longer indicated a small edition of the " ship "—indeed she was often bigger—but implied a vessel of three or more masts, square rigged on all but the aftermost one, which carried fore-and-aft canvas. Most barques were three or four masted, and were very handy vessels in every respect. The smaller sail area on the aftermost mast made little difference to their speed, as was often proved by " ships " which had been converted into " barques " in order to economise in manpower.

An even smaller crew could handle the barquentine, a sailing vessel of three or more masts, square rigged on the foremast only and

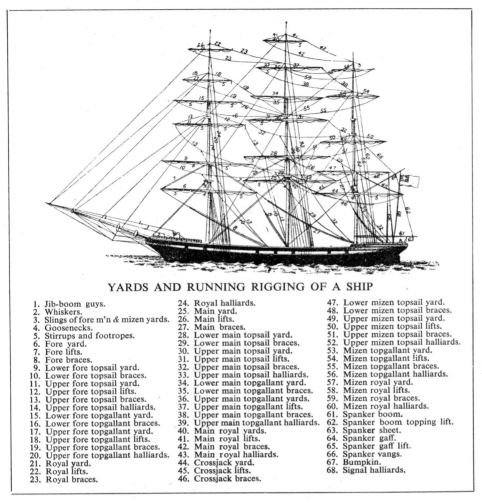

YARDS AND RUNNING RIGGING OF A SHIP

1. Jib-boom guys.
2. Whiskers.
3. Slings of fore m'n & mizen yards.
4. Goosenecks.
5. Stirrups and footropes.
6. Fore yard.
7. Fore lifts.
8. Fore braces.
9. Lower fore topsail yard.
10. Lower fore topsail braces.
11. Upper fore topsail yard.
12. Upper fore topsail lifts.
13. Upper fore topsail braces.
14. Upper fore topsail halliards.
15. Lower fore topgallant yard.
16. Lower fore topgallant braces.
17. Upper fore topgallant yard.
18. Upper fore topgallant lifts.
19. Upper fore topgallant braces.
20. Upper fore topgallant halliards.
21. Royal yard.
22. Royal lifts.
23. Royal braces.
24. Royal halliards.
25. Main yard.
26. Main lifts.
27. Main braces.
28. Lower main topsail yard.
29. Lower main topsail braces.
30. Upper main topsail yard.
31. Upper main topsail lifts.
32. Upper main topsail braces.
33. Upper main topsail halliards.
34. Lower main topgallant yard.
35. Lower main topgallant braces.
36. Upper main topgallant yards.
37. Upper main topgallant lifts.
38. Upper main topgallant braces.
39. Upper main topgallant halliards.
40. Main royal yards.
41. Main royal lifts.
42. Main royal braces.
43. Main royal halliards.
44. Crossjack yard.
45. Crossjack lifts.
46. Crossjack braces.
47. Lower mizen topsail yard.
48. Lower mizen topsail braces.
49. Upper mizen topsail yard.
50. Upper mizen topsail lifts.
51. Upper mizen topsail braces.
52. Upper mizen topsail halliards.
53. Mizen topgallant yard.
54. Mizen topgallant lifts.
55. Mizen topgallant braces.
56. Mizen topgallant halliards.
57. Mizen royal yard.
58. Mizen royal lifts.
59. Mizen royal braces.
60. Mizen royal halliards.
61. Spanker boom.
62. Spanker boom topping lift.
63. Spanker sheet.
64. Spanker gaff.
65. Spanker gaff lift.
66. Spanker vangs.
67. Bumpkin.
68. Signal halliards.

Diagrams reproduced from the " Manual of Seamanship," by permission of H.M. Stationery Office.

with fore-and-aft canvas on the others. With the wind in the right direction she was just as fast as the barque, but on a long voyage she generally lost a lot of time in comparison.

The brig, a two-masted vessel, square rigged on both, was a smaller counterpart of the ship. Slightly different again was the snow, having a small auxiliary mast abaft the mainmast on which the fore-and-aft " spanker " sail was carried. Most of the sailing vessels bringing coal to the London River were brigs and they were generally clumsy and slow, although the rig was not always associated with slow vessels and some brigs had tremendous sail area. Among these were the privateers, the slavers, and the naval brigs used for scouting

[*Nautical.*

TOPSAIL SCHOONER, "ROB ROY," AT SEA

and carrying despatches; they were given such a dangerous amount of sail, and capsized so often, that they were called "coffin" brigs.

The brigantine, a rig originally adapted for piratical purposes but later used principally on the coast, bore the same relation to the brig as the barquentine did to the barque; she was a two-masted vessel, square rigged on the foremast and fore-and-aft rigged on the main.

The schooners were entirely fore-and-aft rigged, although they might carry square topsails between yards on their foremasts. The schooner was a vessel of two or more masts, more or less of equal height and all fore-and-aft rigged, and was the most economical type of sailing ship known. For example, the famous American schooner *Wyoming* carried 5,000 tons of coal with a crew of only twelve men, including the wireless operator.

Schooners could have two or more masts. One of them, the American schooner *Thomas W. Lawson* had no less than seven—and must have been one of the ugliest ships afloat. Generally, of course, the schooner was a very graceful rig and they are still to be found in various parts of the world, fishing or trading in coastal waters.

SAILING SHIPS AND THEIR RIGS

Below the schooners come the rigs with two masts of unequal height ; the ketch, where the short mizen is half the height of the mainmast, and the yawl—now used only in yachts—where the mizen sail is very small indeed. Single masted rigs include the cutter and sloop, formerly used for trading round the coast but now only for pleasure purposes.

The Thames barge, the last remaining sailing type of which numbers may still be seen in the Thames, differs from the others in that her mainsail does not lower but is supported by a sprit, or heavy diagonal boom secured to the foot of the mast. These vessels are really of remarkable beauty and the extraordinary manner in which their expert crews handle them is evident daily. Pre-war the Barge Race was an annual event on London River. They are the most economical type of cargo carrier afloat, some of them carrying several hundred tons of cargo with only two men and a boy.

We have seen how the rig of the bigger sailing ships gradually grew more elaborate, but the time came when this policy was changed by the advent of the steamship. Now, the continued existence of

[*Nautical*

BRIGANTINE, "GILPIN," MAKING SAIL LEAVING PORT

119

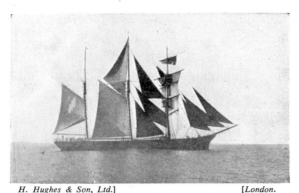

H. Hughes & Son, Ltd.]   [London.

A BARQUENTINE
(The square foresail is furled.)

the sailing vessel depended upon economy. She could not compete for speed but had to rely on the fact that, being driven by wind instead of coal, she could carry cargo more cheaply. It became essential to cut down the size of crew to the minimum and this led to modified rigs. Some of the biggest sails, first the topsail and then the top gallant, were subdivided by an extra yard, and thus were lighter to handle and required fewer men. The new arrangement was called the upper and lower topsail or upper and lower topgallant. Studding sails were abolished, the ship rig practically disappeared except for training vessels, and many ships were reduced to barques ; as an additional economy some big cargo carriers were built with no canvas above their topgallants.

It was the same among the smaller types. The brig and snow required too many men to carry coal down the coast in competition with the steamers. The brigantine and barquentine were more economical, and maintained most—not all —of the brig's advantages for the work. But soon they also were too expensive and gave way to schooners and barges with the smallest possible crews.

Symonds]   [Portsmouth.

A TRAINING BRIG

The sail area has been cut down considerably to make it more easily handled by the boys.

SAILING SHIPS AND THEIR RIGS

[*Nautical.*

"CUTTY SARK," THE FAMOUS OLD CHINA CLIPPER WHICH BROKE ALL
SPEED RECORDS IN THE SEVENTIES AND EIGHTIES
She is now moored off Greenhithe, and used for Training purposes by the Thames Nautical Training College.

The principles of the sailing ship's rig having been made plain, the principles of her rigging follow logically. Every name goes by the mast and the sail. Four masts are the normal maximum and are named fore, main, mizen and jigger ; when there are more than four masts the vessel is a freak and there is then no standard system of naming them—in one famous ship they were named after the days of the week ! It has been mentioned how masts grew taller with the demand for extra sails ; this was achieved by fitting them in sections. The original mast was named the lower mast ; to which was added the topmast—" fidded " on to it with an overlap. Then came the top-gallant mast and finally the royal mast.

The masts are kept standing by means of shrouds to the sides of the ship. These are connected by ratlines, or short lengths of rope which form ladders for the men to go aloft. The fore-and-aft strain is taken by stays, which not only support the mast but offer facilities for setting additional canvas in the form of staysails. Each stay is named after the section of mast it supports, and which in its turn is named after the sail set on it.

The shrouds and stays form the principal part of the " standing rigging ", which is necessary for the ship's safety and remains in position so long as she is rigged. There is also the " running rigging ' which moves according to the way in which the sails are set. Among the running rigging the principal ropes are the halyards, or haulyards, which explains their purpose of hauling the yards and sails into place. On square sails the braces are attached to the ends of the yards, called the yard-arms, and are used for hauling the yard round until the sail is correctly trimmed. The ropes securing the lower corners of a sail are the sheets and in a fore-and-aft vessel slacking out the sheet allows the sail to run out and do its work when the wind is right aft ; when the ship wants to sail as near the wind as possible, the sheet is " close-hauled."

There are, of course, other spars and ropes which have not been mentioned. Each one has its purpose and is repeated for each sail in the ship. When that purpose is understood and the system of naming sails is mastered, it is easy to give every rope its right name.

A. H. Hawke]   *[Helston.*

WRECKED ON THE LIZARD

A CONVOY AT SEA
[*Fox Photos.*

MERCHANTMEN AT WAR

ON the 3rd of September, 1939, the liner *Athenia* was sunk in the Atlantic by an enemy U-boat. That was the beginning of things at sea, the start of a ruthless war that was waged against our merchant shipping throughout the duration of the Second World War.

Submarines, aircraft, surface raiders and warships of all types continually menaced our shipping. We suffered enormous losses. 2,800 British ships were destroyed, representing something like twelve million tons of shipping. No sea was safe ; the main seaports in every belligerent area were heavily attacked from the air ; magnetic and acoustic mines were laid in harbour approaches.

Yet the ships came and went. Grey and dirty and battle-scarred, they continued to supply the sinews of war wherever these were needed. Proud liners raced across oceans carrying thousands of troops ; humble tramps plodded along with their loads of guns, tanks, 'planes and ammunition. Try as he might, the enemy never succeeded in cutting off our vital food supplies.

MERCHANTMEN AT WAR

First credit for all this must go to the Royal Navy, whose gigantic task it was to guard our merchant ships. They did a wonderful job, and no man in the Merchant Navy will ever forget some of their deeds; how the gallant destroyer *Cossack* rescued those British seamen from the prison-ship *Altmark*: how the armed-merchant-cruiser *Jervis Bay*, flying the white ensign, steamed out to engage the overwhelming fire of the *Admiral Scheer* in order that her convoy should have the chance to scatter and survive; how the memorable St. Nazaire raid denied the battleship *Tirpitz* a vital base from which to prey on Atlantic shipping. Nor will the Merchant Navy forget the Royal Air Force and the countless times our airmen drove off or destroyed the enemy's 'planes.

There was, of course, another factor—the courage and determination of the sailormen in our merchant ships. We all know some of their stories, stirring tales like that of the *San Demetrio*, the crippled oil-tanker that was nevertheless re-boarded and somehow brought home by her crew. Such stories made headlines —and films—and have been told already. But perhaps not enough is known of the way in which the war affected the ordinary, everyday lives of our merchant seamen.

From the outset everything was altered and different. The movements of all ships came under Admiralty control. Their peace-time colouring, even their names, were painted over a dull grey; they carried anti-submarine and anti-aircraft guns; unless they were fast ships and ordered to sail " independently " they went in convoy.

On a bright, clear day at sea those convoys were a splendid sight. Forty to sixty merchant ships, steaming along in eight or nine columns and " keeping station " on the commodore ship, which generally led the centre column. Gaily coloured flags fluttered in the breeze as coded signals passed from ship to ship; creamy foam appeared at every stern as they carried out a zigzag, altering course to port or starboard in almost perfect unison. Ahead, out on the flanks or moving hither and thither as necessary would be the escorting warships; overhead, fighter aircraft patrolled the skies.

At once a warlike and yet a peaceful scene. On board each ship some were going about their ordinary duties while others strained watchful eye and ear; the guns were loaded and manned; below decks, engineers kept wary glance not only on bearings and pressure-gauges but on the volume of smoke they were making—because it needed no more than a tell-tale smudge on the horizon to disclose the convoy's presence to a lurking pack of U-boats.

At night there was black-out more complete than any city ever knew. There had to be. A glimmer of light from a porthole could lead to disaster. Station-keeping became a matter of judging by experience your distance from the next vague shape, although in certain weather conditions dimmed navigation lights might be necessary to avoid collisions.

AERIAL ATTACK ON A CONVOY

As the " Focke-Wulfe Kondor " approached, " Hurricane " fighters were catapulted from the deck of merchant vessels.

At the height of the struggle, after France fell and when Italy was still in the war, the Royal Navy was so hard-pressed that convoy protection was sometimes limited. Nevertheless the convoys came through, some unscathed, others less fortunate. The U-boats located and shadowed them, waiting their opportunity. Invariably they sought to attack without warning ; indeed, a heavy vibration through your ship might well be the first hint that some other vessel in the convoy had been torpedoed. You knew then ; even as you rushed hurriedly to " action stations " the unlucky one, if badly holed, might be heeling over and about to sink. Or, loaded perhaps with petrol, she might be a sheet of flame from stem to stern.

The convoy steamed on, or obeyed emergency orders. Those survivors struggling in the water or hanging on to a life-raft would, if humanly possible, be picked up by the special rescue ship attached to the convoy or by one of the escort. No other merchant ship must stop and thus render herself doubly liable to attack. Now would come numerous heavy vibrations as the escort vessels depth-charged the area, hoping for a U-boat " kill." The merest suspicion of anything resembling a periscope brought the thunder and roll of gunfire. A convoy defending itself was the grandest sight. At night, with tracer-bullets flying about, it was like a firework display.

That was the life in convoy, and why it was so necessary for our Merchant Navy sailors quickly to adapt themselves to war-time conditions. The response was magnificent, touching every rank. Your young third officer, perforce trained only by the briefest gunnery course, became immensely proud of his 4-inch gun's crew. With shining eyes he would tell you that the deck-boy was making a first-rate " sightsetter." The cook was coming along, too. As for the bos'n's mate—well, he could load a gun with anyone.

There were anxious times for the shipmaster. It is one thing to sail in convoy in fair weather ; in dense fog or a howling gale the near proximity of fifty other ships is a troublesome thought. Yet, as always, humorous situations could arise. One shipmaster, perhaps with undue pride in his own ability to keep station, would, every morning, survey the rest of the convoy through glasses and comment in no uncertain terms upon such as were out of position. One night, due to earlier enemy action and a consequent change of route, their convoy crossed the track of an outward bound one. There were some close shaves as the two convoys manœuvered clear and then the various shapes re-formed themselves and continued on.

At daybreak, the same shipmaster looked about him and began making his usual comments. Suddenly he frowned. " I don't recognize that ship," he told his chief officer. " Nor that one . . . nor . . . " and there his voice trailed off as he suddenly realized that, in the dark and confusion, his ship had somehow re-formed into the wrong convoy !

There were, of course, all manner of convoys. Those to Russia, when frightful and freezing weather conditions were added to the hazards of war. And who could forget the Malta convoys, taking food and ammunition and petrol to that hard-pressed island garrison? Small, fast convoys these, heavily escorted. Atlantic convoys might or might not be attacked. If you were bound for Malta you were certain of repeated and prolonged attack from sea and air. Wave after wave of aircraft—dive-bombing attacks, low-level and high-level bombing attacks, torpedo-

[Fox Photos.

SHIPS OF ALL SHAPES AND SIZES
The convoy stretched out as far as the eye can reach.

bombing attacks—submarines, surface craft, they all came time and again, night and day. And near misses were far too frequent to count.

And there were the landings—from the first North African ones to the equally successful Normandy ones. Armadas of merchant ships took part in them all, and their sailormen were glad to be there. These were the hard-won fruits of victory. In helping to achieve it, many thousands of their comrades had been lost at sea and they were right to take pride in being part of those splendid offensive ventures through which our fighting services won the way to freedom.

The ill-fated beautiful luxury Royal Mail liner "Magdalena," which ran aground off the Brazilian coast on her maiden trip and broke in two as she was being towed into Rio harbour.

[Fox Photos.

A BUSY SCENE IN THE KING GEORGE V DOCK, LONDON

THE FIRST CLASS LOUNGE, UNION CASTLE ROYAL MAILS M.V. "CAPETOWN CASTLE"

LIFE IN A LINER

ANYONE who finds a voyage—even a very long one—in a modern passenger steamer dull, must be hard to please. It matters little where you go—to the Land of the Midnight Sun ; to the Mediterranean ; to the Far East ; or westward to the great American continent—in all cases the steamship companies will do their best to make you perfectly comfortable, to feed you well, and to give you every possible pleasure.

When you embark, the most important official, so far as you are concerned, is not the captain—that high and mighty dignitary has quite enough to do without looking after the passengers personally —but the chief steward of that portion of the vessel (first, cabin, or tourist) you are travelling in. After inspecting your ticket, he will assign you a place at table, and it is understood that you will occupy that place at every meal. Other stewards will direct you to your stateroom, or cabin, and wait upon you at table. You will find, indeed, that the service and attention given to you in a passenger liner is equalled only in the best and most luxurious hotels ashore.

The picture on pages 24-5, sectional view of the famous Cunard White Star vessel *Queen Mary*, shows how the decks of a great liner are arranged. It will be seen that nearly the whole of the ship is given over to the passengers, to the store-rooms, mail-rooms, and the various engines. The space available for cargo is very small considering the size of the vessels, and is occupied principally by light goods for which rapid transit is necessary. The engines and the boiler-rooms also occupy a great deal of space, but in modern oil-burning liners considerable space formerly needed for coal is now saved.

FIRST CLASS CABIN DINING SALOON R.M.S. "PRETORIA CASTLE"

In the newer Transatlantic boats there are lifts, or elevators, which connect most of the main passenger decks and save you the trouble of ascending or descending the staircases. The attendant will stop at any "floor," just as he would in a hotel or a large shop.

In the intermediate types of passenger steamships, and these are the great majority, the public rooms are naturally fewer and much less spacious, but the passengers are not less comfortable on that account. By night and day electric fans and concealed pipes draw the vitiated air from the cabins and public rooms, replacing it by invigorating fresh sea air, and in cold weather the incoming air is warmed. In the *Queen Mary*, the first-class staterooms are provided with a ventilation system which allows the individual passenger to control the amount of warm or cold air entering his room. The increase in the size of ships has made for more spacious cabins, and there are also very often suites of rooms like small flats, so that

THE LONG GALLERY, UNION CASTLE R.M.M.V. "CAPETOWN CASTLE" (27000 tons)

wealthy passengers can secure as much privacy as they care to pay for. Solid silver fittings, silk tapestries and curtains, the best of carpets, and the most artistic furniture are provided. Many of the cabins and all the suites have their own lavatory accommodation and bathroom, with hot and cold water laid on. Bedside telephones are sometimes installed, and the largest liners have a telephone exchange with facilities making it possible for passengers to have world-wide telephone calls.

LIFE IN A LINER

For leisure hours there are well-supplied libraries, smoking-rooms, music-rooms, and lounges or drawing-rooms, though in no two ships, even those belonging to the same owners, are these apartments quite alike. The sumptuousness and luxury of modern passenger vessels surprise people who are travelling for the first time. The giant *Queen Mary*, for instance, which splendid and marvellous vessel has been aptly described as " the city which goes to sea," is the last word in modern luxury and comfort. Like her sister, the *Queen Elizabeth*, and other large liners, she has a veritable street of fascinating shops, and even a bank.

The work of many famous artists contributes to the magnificence of the interior decoration of such liners, with their beautiful carvings and paintings. Timber from every corner of the British Commonwealth went into the panelling and other woodwork of the *Mauretania*. British liners used often to go in for " period " furnishing in their public rooms, and many excellent and pleasing reproductions were achieved. Now, however, " period " furnishing has been largely abandoned in favour of more modern styles with the emphasis upon brightness. Among the figured woods, ash, chestnut, and bleached mahogany, are extensively used in furniture and panelling. Plastics, also, play a prominent part.

Formerly, large liners divided their accommodation into first, second, and third-class. Then, for some years, the first-class was often called " cabin " and the second-class was referred to as " tourist," third-class remaining unchanged in name. Now, although companies differ somewhat, the tendency is to name them " First-class," " Cabin," and " Tourist," thus doing away altogether with the old third-class.

The food on board is excellent, and menus offer a bewildering choice. The dining-rooms are splendidly appointed and seat many hundreds. The *Queen Mary's* magnificent dining-room—or Main Restaurant—is one of the largest rooms built into a vessel. It is 118 feet broad, 160 feet long, and rises in tiers to a height of thirty feet.

The sleeping-cabins in a liner, and even in much smaller new ships, contain most comfortable beds instead of the former bunks. Many are arranged with bedsteads exactly as ashore. Privacy is secured by placing only one or two persons in each sleeping-cabin ; there is, indeed, a marked tendency to increase the number of single-berth cabins, and of course all cabins are now splendidly decorated and

AN UNUSUAL VIEW OF THE "AQUITANIA" AT SEA

133

THE COCKTAIL BAR "EMPRESS OF
CANADA"
A Canadian Pacific Liner

furnished. There is, indeed, every possible comfort and requirement in a modern liner's stateroom. There are large built-in wardrobes, sometimes even with interior illumination. Soft carpets and rugs cover the floor; there is ingenious strip lighting on the walls, besides dressing-table and bed-side lamps. Contrast all this luxury with the old narrow, shelf-like bunk with "preventer boards" wedged in, to keep you from falling out during an extra heavy roll.

In the morning the bed-room stewards knock at your door and tell you it is time to get up, perhaps bringing a cup of tea or coffee and a dainty biscuit, a little attention most grown-up people appreciate at sea. A turn or two on deck gives a splendid appetite for break-fast, which will be finished by nine or ten o'clock.

Meals may be announced by the ship's bugler, who takes his stand at different parts of the vessel in rotation. Some-times the military call is given, sometimes the bugler indulges in fanfares which half a dozen cars could not surpass; his appearance is the signal that dinner, or other meal, is ready— that is the principal considera-tion. Lunch is served about one and afternoon tea at four.

A CORNER OF THE SMOKING ROOM
(R.M.M.V. "CAPETOWN CASTLE")

LIFE IN A LINER

There are many ways in which passengers pass the rest of their time. Promenading the spacious decks is a favourite form of exercise. When you wish to sit down, the deck steward will hasten to supply you with a deck lounge and cushions. A deck chair is usually hired in advance for the voyage. The speed of the ship is a never-failing source of conversation every morning, and most passengers take a share in the many guessing competitions which are arranged, prizes being given to those who most nearly guess the number of miles covered each day. Some passengers make friends with the engine-room staff, and try to learn whether there have been any variations in the speed, but this is not fair, and is really useless, as only the navigating officer can know the nature of the adverse or favourable currents the ship may have experienced. The day's run is generally posted up at the head of the grand staircase or, in some other conspicuous place, where an expectant little group of passengers will probably be waiting to learn their luck. The figures are announced as soon after the captain has "taken the sun" as they can be computed.

FIRST CLASS LOUNGE OF THE CANADIAN PACIFIC LINER "EMPRESS OF CANADA"

"Eight bells," calls the captain, and immediately a sailor in attendance gives the ship's bell four pairs of strokes. This is noon, and the ship's time will be regulated from it until next midday. If you are travelling to the east you will find that you have to put your watch ahead each day to keep time with the ship, but if you are westward bound your watch will be fast. Thus, in crossing the 180th meridian eastward in the Pacific, you will have a week of eight days, but only one of six days if you are travelling westward.

FIRST CLASS SWIMMING POOL, "BRITANNIC"

Cricketers are enabled to indulge in their favourite game on a coco-nut matting pitch, with nets to prevent the ball from falling into the sea. Some passengers like to take exercise in the gymnasium or on the rowing machines.

Deck quoits, too, are a favourite amusement. There are several ways of playing. One is to attempt to throw the rope rings or quoits on to pegs ; another is to drop them into squares chalked on the deck ; a third method is to try which side can get the most quoits nearest to a single chalk mark. Quoits give a good deal of fun, as the rolling of the vessel, and sometimes the wind, have to be allowed for, and the best player ashore is not always the best afloat. Shovel-board, or shuffle-board, is generally popular, and can best be described as a half-way game between shove-halfpenny and curling. Those who like something more boisterous can indulge in the events of the gymkhana, which usually provoke screams of laughter from start to finish. There are wheelbarrow races with human " barrows " who may or may not have roller skates on their hands for the wheels ;

and obstacle races, with a sail full of water for one of the obstacles and swinging barrels for another. In spar fights the contestants straddle a spar and belabour each other with pillows, footballs, old newspapers, or anything else easy to wield and not likely to hurt much, until one or other of the players falls off into a sail of water. Leap-frog is played with rules not observed on shore, and there are potato races, cork and spoon races, and many other events. Skipping matches, too, are generally popular.

The musically inclined are sure to find in the music-room some kindred spirits. On every ocean-going steamer a concert in aid of one of the seamen's charities is got up at least once every voyage —perhaps for the Seamen's Orphanage, or the Life-boat Institution.

A tour of inspection of the ship is always interesting, but it must be remembered that certain places like the navigating bridge and the engine-rooms are out of bounds for obvious reasons.

In some of the largest liners there is a cinema—the *Queen Mary* possessing one that seats 200 persons, while the *Queen Elizabeth* has one seating 338 persons. Both are air-conditioned and specially designed for good acoustics.

Most liners make special provision for dancing and the larger ones

CHILDREN'S PLAYROOM (CUNARD WHITE STAR LINER)

often engage some well-known dance orchestra to play in the ballroom, where a gay atmosphere is created by colour-change lighting and suitable decorations.

Fancy-dress balls and other dances are greatly enjoyed on deck in the evenings while passing through the tropics, and no end of fun is caused when the costumes to be worn are

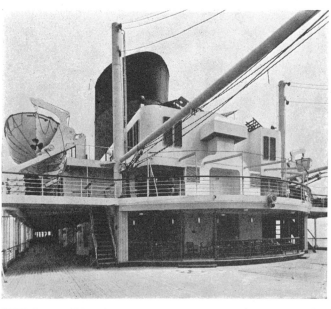

THE SUPERSTRUCTURES AND FUNNEL ON THE R.M.S. LINER " PRETORIA CASTLE " ARE STREAMLINED TO ELIMINATE WIND RESISTANCE

decided by ballot and have to be improvised in a given time.

The ports at which the steamers call are never-failing sources of interest, and there is often time to go ashore for an hour or two. A great deal can be learnt, too, by comparing the different boats and boatmen at the various ports. The Moors still use surf-boats of the type so useful to them when they were known as " the scourge of the Mediterranean " ; in the Red Sea you will find the Arabs using what is believed to be the oldest type of sea-going open boat ; and at Bombay and Colombo you will make the acquaintance of canoes, both single and with outriggers. Farther East still are sampans and junks, such as those shown in our pictures elsewhere.

Should the vessel be crossing tropical seas, there are the flying fish and nautilus to be noted, and often you may see dolphins and porpoises showing how fast they can swim. In the waters off Central America, and elsewhere, you may one day find the calm, blue sea dotted with hundreds of rather flat and brightly shining objects which look at first like so many mirrors reflecting the sun's rays. They will be turtles, giant cousins of the tortoise you may have kept at home. During disturbed tropical weather, you may see that curious phenomenon known as a water-spout.

Sometimes, though rarely nowadays, you may see one of the most beautiful sights in the world, a large, full-rigged sailing ship, or a four-masted barque, bowling along before the trade wind, with every inch of sail set, her canvas gleaming white in the sunlight or reflecting the ever-varying hues of the tropical sunsets. Nor can you miss those sunsets at sea in the Tropics; no one can describe their beauty; they are alone worth making a voyage to gaze upon and to marvel at.

Then, also, in southern waters you may see the albatrosses and other beautiful sea-birds. The albatross has very large wings, which sometimes measure as much as fifteen feet from tip to tip when they are spread for flying. It has been said that an albatross can sleep on the wing, and certainly at times these huge and graceful birds seem to be floating along in the air with scarcely a movement to show that they are flying. No seafaring man harms them, because there is

CUNARD WHITE STAR LINER " MEDEA "
From the air.

Photo] CATAMARANS AT MADRAS [Bourne & Shepherd.

an old superstition which says that the souls of sailors drowned at sea enter the bodies of sea-birds.

To have, as passenger, a good time at sea, be thoughtful for the convenience of all with whom you come in contact; don't expect impossibilities from the stewards; help your fellow-travellers to enjoy themselves; and you will be astonished at the number of friendships you will have made and how much pleasure you have derived by the time the voyage is ended.

ROYAL MAIL CRUISING LINER "ATLANTIS"

THE LIGHTSHIP BREAKSEA

This well-known lightship is moored in the Bristol Channel. It shows a white electric light giving one flash of 0.5 second every 15 seconds. The light has a candle power of 300,000 and is visible at a distance of eleven miles in clear weather. A Diaphone fog signal gives blasts of 2 seconds every 20 seconds.

THE SAILOR'S SIGNPOSTS

JUST as when you go for a walk or a bicycle ride in country that you do not know, you take your direction largely from signposts and prominent objects, so do those who go down to the sea in ships, though their signposts are very different, and to landsmen at first a little puzzling.

You can readily understand that a ship on a voyage must at all times be able to ascertain her exact position on the chart. If she is in the middle of an ocean out of sight of land, the captain or other officer finds out where the vessel is by the use of an instrument known as a sextant (illustration on page 209), though it would take too long to explain here exactly how this is done. When approaching coastlines he invariably employs a recording device such as the Admiralty pattern echo-sounder.

Here, in fact, the problem becomes more difficult. Not only has the captain to recognize the particular section of coastline the ship has reached, but he must navigate his vessel along that coastline to the mouth of the harbour for which he is bound, when usually he will hand over the navigation to a pilot. Lighthouses, lightships, buoys and beacons were invented and are maintained in order to enable him to do this in safety.

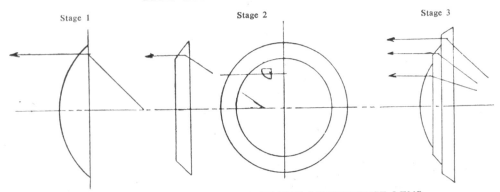

Stage 1   Stage 2   Stage 3

STAGES IN THE EVOLUTION OF THE LIGHTHOUSE LENS

When first Man began to venture forth on the water without the friendly aid of daylight to guide him home, his friends on land assisted him by lighting flares on the shore from which he had ventured. The early maritime nations of the Mediterranean went a step further, and some of them had lights to mark the entrances to their harbours, such as the famous Pharos of Alexandria, which, with a height of nearly 400 feet, is reputed to have cast a smoky sulphurous glare which could be seen nearly forty miles away. The Romans introduced coast lights into Great Britain in the form of stone towers, on the top of which wood or other fires were lighted ; remains of such towers may be seen on parts of the coast to this day. Little progress was made for hundreds of years after the Romans left our islands; even so recently as 1812 in certain parts there were still so-called coast lights that were simply copies of the primitive Roman fire towers. Now and again attempts were made to enclose the fire on top of the tower in order to concentrate the beams ; some people even tried placing a piece of polished brass be-hind the fire with the idea of

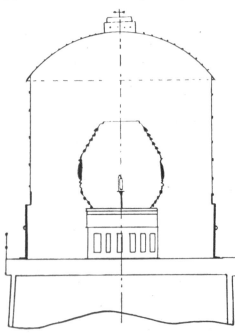

CROSS-SECTION OF A LIGHTHOUSE LANTERN AND LANTERN HOUSE
The lantern is built on the Fresnel system.

142

reflecting the flame. As a matter of fact, this crude idea really led to the first types of lighthouse apparatus, in which tallow candles were employed as the source of illumination. The candles were placed at the focus of a highly polished metallic mirror, shaped somewhat like the scooped-out end of an egg. Such a mirror, with certain fixed mathematical properties, is known as a parabolic mirror, and in conjunction with oil lamps or gas mantles is used in many lighthouses and lightships at the present day.

The first real step in modern lighthouse engineering was taken in 1811, when Augustus Fresnel, a French scientist, applied the ordinary bull's-eye lens, of "bull's-eye lantern" fame, to the reflection of light on a large scale. He found that when he wanted to use a powerful apparatus his bull's-eye was too cumbersome, so he adopted an ingenious method of overcoming the difficulty. Taking his bull's-eye, he cut it into longitudinal slices parallel with the flat side. Each slice he made a little smaller in diameter than it had been, then he cut out a smaller ring still from each of the diminished slices. Thus he was left with a very small bull's-eye, and with a number of rings like those shown in the figure on page 142. He fitted these in position and, as you will see, there had the genesis of the modern lighthouse lantern, which is apt to appear so confusing to the seaside visitor who, after a stiff climb up stone stairs and a narrow escape from knocking his head off on a steel beam, emerges into the lantern-room of a lighthouse.

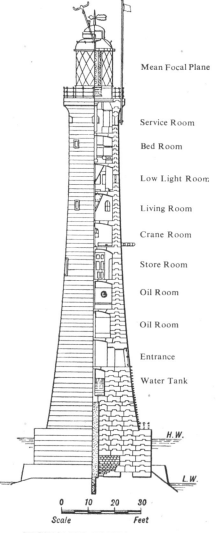

Mean Focal Plane

Service Room

Bed Room

Low Light Room

Living Room

Crane Room

Store Room

Oil Room

Oil Room

Entrance

Water Tank

H.W.

L.W.

0 10 20 30

Scale   Feet

SECTIONAL ELEVATION OF
EDDYSTONE LIGHTHOUSE

Showing arrangement of rooms one above the other

When situated close to a town, the modern lighthouse operates from current generated by the local power station, but most lighthouses are on remote parts of coastline and these have their own power house.

The source of light at the focus of the lens apparatus just described was originally an oil lamp, then became a petroleum pressure burner and is now an electric filament lamp. A standby lamp is also fitted within the lens and this comes into focus and lights-up automatically in the event of the lamp in focus burning-out.

By courtesy of]   [Chance Brothers & Co. Ltd.

MODERN ELECTRIC LIGHTHOUSE LENS APPARATUS

Light from the lamp is then condensed (by the lens) into "spokes" of light which point to the horizon in such a way as to appear as flashes to the mariner when the lens is rotated. The lens is rotated by an electric motor, and if this should fail, a standby motor comes into operation automatically.

Lighthouses must never fail to give their warning and guiding beams, and electricity is provided by a generator driven by a diesel engine. If a fault in the engine causes it to fail, the generator is shut down automatically and a bell rings continuously—waking the keeper, and will not stop ringing until he has started a standby generating plant. Three generating plants are employed so that two generating plants may fail without the lighthouse being put out of operation.

A lighthouse operating by push-button control may sound rather fantastic but, in fact, the generating plants are started and stopped by push-buttons. As soon as it gets dark, a photo-electric switch rings the alarm bell which will not stop ringing until the keeper has put the lighthouse into operation. If the keeper attempts to douse the lighthouse before day-break, the bell rings again until he re-lights !

Another great advantage is that the keeper can have a good night's sleep if nothing goes wrong because the light-house operates automatically during the night.

Various types of lighthouse are in use to-day. First of all, there are large and important lights like the Eddystone, the Wolf Rock, and the Bishop Rock off the south-west coast of Great Britain, or the Fastnet Rock off the south-west corner of Ireland. These are known as " rock lights," because they are built upon rocky reefs, and their construction was a tremendously difficult task, a long battle, in fact, against elements. As you will see

By courtesy of]   *[Messrs. Chance Bros. & Co., Ltd.*

PORT SAID LIGHTHOUSE

A large modern lighthouse apparatus. This goes inside the outer lantern. On the right is the operating motor. Note the size compared with the man.

[James Gibson.

ROUND ISLAND LIGHTHOUSE, ISLES OF SCILLY

from the pictures they are tall, graceful, tapering, circular structures, made of large stone blocks dovetailed into each other and cemented together, the whole structure being firmly dovetailed into the solid rock. The structure is solid masonry for about a third of the way up; then, behind a wall of tremendous thickness, are arranged the living rooms for the keepers, storehouses for provisions and for the

[James Gibson.

THE LIVING ROOM IN THE BISHOP ROCK LIGHTHOUSE, SITUATED OFF THE SCILLY ISLES oil which is burned in the lantern; and lastly, but not least, on top of all is the big metal structure of the lantern itself. These rock lights are exposed to the very worst weather and sometimes it is impossible to relieve the keepers until long after the normal end of their duty period. Even then, boarding the relief boat may be no simple matter.

Outward bound, a ship's departure is generally taken from a well-known rock light; homeward bound, eager eyes seek the lighthouse marking the return to the home coast. The Fastnet Rock Light, off the Irish coast, is a favourite departure point for ships crossing the

[Graphic Photo Union.

EDDYSTONE LIGHTHOUSE

Atlantic, and the Bishop Rock Light, on one of the outcrops of the Scilly Isles, is a favourite return mark. Sailors term such lighthouses " landfall lights " and include any prominent lighthouse which may be so used. Thus, a landfall light may be situated on a headland, notable examples being on the famous and treacherous Lizard Head and on St. Catherine's Head in the Isle of Wight, both of which are electric and ranking among the most powerful lights in the world.

A lighthouse would be of little use—or even dangerous—if the navigator had any doubt about its identity and for this reason no two lighthouses in the same locality are similar in appearance. At night, as any chart will show, lighthouses in relative proximity exhibit lights of a character so different that there can be no mistake.

COAST LIGHTS AND HARBOUR LIGHTS

Having made our landfall, we proceed along the coast and find that lighthouses are placed on most of the headlands ; they are powerful, but not quite so powerful as the landfall lights. Lighthouses like those at Beachy Head and Dungeness are examples of coast lights. Then, as we reach our destination, we come to such a variety of types and kinds of lights and channel marks that it is difficult to classify them simply. We can roughly divide ports and harbours into two groups, those which stand on big broad estuarine rivers, or arms of the sea, like London, Liverpool, Glasgow and Southampton, and those which stand on comparatively narrow rivers like the ports of Newcastle or Middlesbrough. In the first case, if the estuary be of a rocky nature, like the Clyde, there will be a number of little lighthouses, some of them designed to work automatically, without continuous attendance, while if the estuary be sandy, like the Thames, there will be small lighthouses built on steel screw piles, and lightships. In the second case, if the river be a narrow one, like the Tyne, there will be two stone piers built out from the shore to mark the river entrance, and on the end of each pier will be a small stone lighthouse.

SANDBANKS

Sandbanks are a very grave danger to ships which run aground on them, because if the ship cannot get off in time it will be broken up by the waves and in time sucked into the sand itself. The famous Goodwin Sands, near Ramsgate, which are continually shifting, are notoriously treacherous. Sandbanks are generally marked either by screw-pile lighthouses or by lightships.

Screw-pile lighthouses are built up with a number of steel tubes, having as their foundation four or more main piles, the bottom ends of which are pointed and shaped somewhat like a corkscrew ; when these have been firmly screwed into the sand the cross strips and the tops of the piles are placed in position and bolted up, then above them is built the house for the keepers, and on top of all is mounted the iron and glass framework for the lantern.

BISHOP ROCK LIGHTHOUSE, ISLES OF SCILLY

SUPPLYING FOOD TO THE WOLF ROCK LIGHTHOUSE BY HELICOPTER

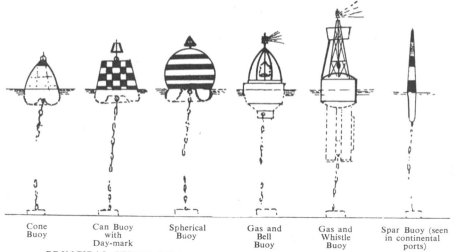

| Cone Buoy | Can Buoy with Day-mark | Spherical Buoy | Gas and Bell Buoy | Gas and Whistle Buoy | Spar Buoy (seen in continental ports) |

PRINCIPAL TYPES OF BUOYS IN HARBOURS AND ESTUARIES

LIGHTSHIPS

Lightships are in many ways the most fascinating part of our subject ; historically, they date from the eighteenth century, when they consisted of small wooden ships moored near the sandbank they were guarding, and having a single mast with a large wooden

[Aerofilms.

THE MERSEY " BAR " LIGHT-VESSEL. THE LOCATING LIGHT FOR THE PORT OF LIVERPOOL

A small screw-pile Lighthouse that stood on the Ness at Lowestoft. Owing to changes in the shape of the foreshore the light had to be removed.

yard, at each end of which a lantern was suspended. Lightships have progressed, and modern vessels are fine seaworthy craft having lights of similar character to land lighthouses and correspondingly powerful. English lightships are painted red, with the name of the sand they guard in large white letters on their sides. They have a tall central lattice tower upon which the lantern is mounted. The apparatus within is electric and is similar to that already described for a lighthouse. The lens is mounted upon a pendulum, however, so that the light-

beams are not disturbed by the rolling of the vessel. If, as sometimes happens, a lightship is driven out of position by exceptionally rough weather she shows special lights to indicate that she is not to be relied upon, and in daytime hoists the flags PC, meaning "Lightvessel out of position."

British lightships do not as a rule have the power of self-propulsion, but American and some Continental lightships are fitted to-day with diesel-

By courtesy of]   [Messrs. Chance Bros. & Co., Ltd.

AN AUTOMATIC FLASHING LIGHT BUOY

It is fitted with a lantern and lens and four cylinders of acetylene gas. Will operate for twelve months without attention.

152

electric drive or by direct coupled internal-combustion engines which can, if necessary, propel them at 6 or 7 knots. All lightships are small strongly built craft, formerly of oak but now invariably of steel; they have to stand a tremendous amount of knocking about and they are moored by stout cables and large anchors shaped exactly like a huge steel umbrella and known accordingly as "umbrella" or "mushroom" anchors. In calm weather passing ships can readily confirm their estimation of how the tide is running by observing which way the lightship is lying. The crews of lightships are periodically relieved for a spell ashore in the same way as lighthouse keepers.

BUOYS

Let us talk briefly about the many-coloured, many-shaped objects seen in the water on either side as you pass up an estuary in a steamer; these are called "buoys," and may be of various types. Smaller buoys mark a channel and may be of three distinct shapes, (a) cone buoys, shaped like a cone above the water-line; (b) can buoys, shaped like an inverted zinc pail above the water-line; and (c) spherical buoys. Types of these are shown in the sketches on page 151.

In Britain, if you are going up one of the river channels from the sea, you will find on your right hand (or starboard) side conical buoys, generally painted red, and on your left hand (or port) side you will find can buoys, painted black or in black and white squares. If there should be a shoal or a shallow patch in the middle of the channel, you will find each end marked by a spherical

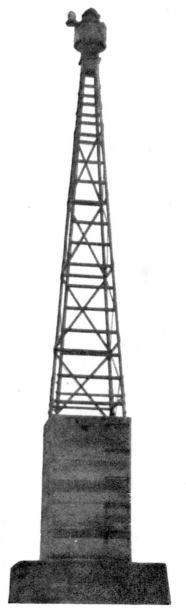

The structure is fitted with a "Chance" light-valve for automatically turning on and extinguishing the light at sunset and sunrise. With four cylinders of gas this light will go for six months unattended.

153

buoy, known usually as a "middle ground" buoy.

Sometimes these channel-marking buoys have a super-structure on which is mounted a lamp fed with gas and arranged to flash automatically until the gas is exhausted. Sometimes, too, they have a distinguishing mark, such as a cone or a triangle. Lighted buoys, as they are sometimes called, are often

[*Topical.*
A CAN BUOY WITH DAY-MARK READY FOR RELEASE

[*Topical.*
FIXING A DAY-MARK ON A CAN BUOY

very large, especially in America, where they become literally young lighthouses, some having a height of nearly 15 feet above the water-line. Many buoys have bells which ring when the buoy rolls in the swell ; others have whistles blown by air compressed in a steel cylinder under the body of the buoy, so that as the buoy rises and falls in the seaway the column of air in the cylinder, directly connected with a whistle, gets bigger or smaller and makes the whistle blow. There are no more eerie sounds than those to be heard when steaming down a channel marked by alternate bell and whistle buoys. As with lighthouses and lightships, nearby buoys have suitably different light characteristics.

FOGS

The sailor's most dreaded enemy is fog. Generally speaking, a fog at sea is much worse than a fog on land. You can't see the land and you certainly can't see any lighthouse or lightship. The obvious thing to do then is to make a warning noise, and that was the beginning of all methods of fog-signalling. To-day we have fog horns, diaphones and sirens operated by compressed air, and in America powerful steam whistles are often used. Explosive signals are also employed.

But these methods suffer from one grave defect, uncertainty. Sound, like light, is propagated in waves, but owing to the sound waves encountering belts of atmosphere of different densities, the sound is distorted and you cannot be certain, if you hear a siren at a mile from the source of sound, that you are going to hear it at two miles away, though you may hear it perfectly again at three miles. However, " noise " methods are used very largely at the present day, both in lighthouses and lightships.

Radar, the principle of which is briefly explained in the article " Wireless at Sea," has extraordinary possibilities as an aid to navigation in fog. Not only are collision risks considerably lessened in ships equipped with radar, but the negotiation of tortuous buoyed channels may be undertaken and it has been demonstrated that large liners can be safely navigated into harbour through dense fog. The invention is being even further developed. At Gladstone Dock, in Liverpool, a Radar tower equipped with six luminous screens is in being and " pictures " the whole of the Mersey out to the Bar lightship, showing ships, buoys and beacons, etc. Shore-based Radar operators can communicate with ships entering or leaving the Mersey, giving them their positions and warning them of danger by radio telephone. Thus it may soon be that ships are literally " talked " into port.

The modern echo sounder is another item of increasing navigational value which can be adapted to fog duties, especially the self-recording type.

"SORRY, TOO ROUGH!"

A Trinity House Relief Steamer signalling a Lightship.

Although the men on lightships are nominally relieved at regular intervals, in rough weather it is frequently too dangerous to put off a small boat. In such cases the light-keepers have to swallow their disappointment, and perhaps wait another long period.

By courtesy of the]

A PEARLING KETCH

[Queensland Government.

THE MYSTERY OF THE LAGOON

THE pearling lugger *Noumea* lay at anchor in a little land-locked bay of the Admiralty Islands in the Western Pacific. It was a sultry, windless day. About the ship the quiet sea lay blue as the heavens above, and round the lagoon, over the white, dazzling beaches, green palms hung listless and silent. Few European ships at that time came to these remote groups. The skipper of the *Noumea* had visited the islands on the chance of finding pearl-banks, of which he had been told by a friendly chief. Besides the captain and a crew of six Line islanders, there were on board two native divers and one white diver, Eliab Fuller, from the Connecticut sea-board, reputed to be the best man at the business in the whole Pacific. He drew eighty-five pounds per month, work or no work, and more than one firm would gladly have paid him even higher wages, for there was no better man at this dangerous trade. It was said that, bar accidents, Fuller could raise twice as much shell as any diver between Manila and the Ducies, and his daring was the talk of every port in the Central Pacific, where bravery is the one common virtue.

Yet that afternoon, as he stood in the bows of the *Noumea's* boat alongside the lugger, Fuller was manifestly ill at ease. In the clear depths far below the shadow of the ship hovered on the pale sea-bottom, and through the unruffled crystal dashed strange and brilliant shapes, among which, occasionally, glided the great rudder fish. But there was an uneasy restlessness amongst these creatures of the deep, as if they apprehended some danger. Heavy rains had fallen the evening before, and, at such times, in some of the islands, the terrible Tanifa shark draws shoreward and infests the land-locked waters. None of these scourges had been sighted ; never-theless, before the helmet was screwed into place, Fuller lingered with a strange foreboding, looking earnestly at the white beaches, the green jags of the palms, and the water purple under the cloudless sky.

" Keep your eyes skinned, boys," he said fretfully, as they adjusted the helmet. " It's kind of unwholesome paying a surprise call in these unknown pockets of sea, and after that lump of rain we had at nightfall it's right here I should look if I wanted to find a Tanifa."

With that, he went heavily over the side.

The water closed above him in green coils, and a flight of bubbles fled upwards before his eyes. He heard the throb of the pumps surging in his ears, and saw the shadow of the ship rise swiftly overhead in the green dim light till, at twenty and odd fathoms, his feet rested on a shoal. The pressure drove the hot blood buzzing behind his eardrums, as he walked about the oozy hollows that spread dreamily under the faint light.

At first he thought he had struck a barren patch, but presently, by the side of a shadowy hollow, he came to a fair quantity of shell. With the speed of practice, he stooped to fill his net-bag, a con-trivance of his own design, and was so busy that he hardly noticed the insidious, numbing effect of the pressure about his heart and the confused roar in his ears.

Some instinct, perhaps a vibration in the water about him, caused him to look quickly behind in the depths beyond the shellbank. Instantly, with a sickening access of terror, he reeled backwards on the yielding bed of the sea.

Far above him, rising swiftly out of the hollow and its tangle of waving weeds, swept a colossal shape, matching the dim water in colour, and seemingly half-transparent. It hung overhead, a monstrous shadow, out of which huge relentless eyes, horribly luminous, glared at the diver, who, for the moment, was paralysed with fear. The creature descended, opening and contracting its vast sack-like mouth, a deep yawning cavity armed with fangs. Suddenly, long snaky tentacles shot out from the huge bulk of the body and enveloped the diver, who had so completely lost his nerve that he did not even attempt to use the signal cord.

The monster was now immediately above the diver, cutting off his retreat upwards ; the great eyes glared almost within touching distance. Some of the tentacles were entangled about the air tube and compressed it, partially cutting off the supply. Fuller already felt the pulsation of the water ejected in streams from the huge gaping mouth. He tried to collect his scattered wits, numbed by the terrible pressure. There was no time to rid himself of the bag of shells at his waist, because already the feelers had twined about his body and the great bulk of the enemy obscured the light.

In the diver's hand was a long, light crowbar of steel, very keen at one end, which he used in his work on the reefs. By a miracle of sudden and cold calculation, he drove the instrument with all his force into one of the great glowing eyes above him, twisting the bar round and round to make the wound more deadly. The weapon plunged into the glaring disk so deeply that the diver's fist was half embedded in the shattered, gelatinous mass.

Swept clean off his feet by the convulsions of his gigantic enemy, Fuller himself never knew clearly what followed. The very depths of the sea were shaken ; he dimly saw a vast mass float upward like a released balloon : burning eyes glittered among a tangle of python-like feelers and vanished. Then suddenly he was jerked to his feet, raised swiftly upwards through the dim green depths, and before unconsciousness blotted out the twilit world of the under-sea, there once more swept by him a vast glassy body, contracting and expanding among a score of long, writhing tentacles, that clutched at him desperately, then sank out of sight into the dim abysses of water.

THE MYSTERY OF THE LAGOON

When he came to, he found himself lying on the planks of the boat in the sunshine, and beheld, with the peculiar relish of one who has come within reach of Death, the blue sky, the beaches glistening under the sun, and the joyous, rippling sea.

It was two days before Fuller recovered from the effects of the mental strain and the terrible pressure. Nevertheless, as soon as he was himself again, he coolly volunteered to explore the spot once more. But the shells he had brought up turned out unproductive, and the skipper refused to permit another attempt in that part of the bay. The shallower waters also yielded such poor results that, within a fortnight, the *Noumea* quitted those islands.

During this time, encouraged by the natives, who reported the occasional appearance of an unknown monster in the lagoon, a careful watch was kept for the submarine terror ; but although those on board the *Noumea* repeatedly explored the reef and the surrounding waters, no trace of it was found, and they were compelled to leave without any further knowledge of its nature.

DUTCH TUG—" ZWARTE ZEE "
One of the world's most powerful tugs.

YACHT RACING IN QUEENSTOWN HARBOUR

[*Nautical.*

YACHTS AND YACHTING

TO describe yachts and yachting in a single short article is difficult, for there are many different kinds of pleasure craft round the coast, and people have very different ideas as to what constitutes a holiday on the water.

At the top of the social tree are the big steam yachts ; these are the monopoly of the rich, for they are not cheap to build and the cost of keeping them up through a season is enormous. Many do not care for this type, considering them merely floating flats, and declaring that their owners have little real love for sailing, and use them simply for moving from one social function to another. This may be true of some steam yacht-owners, but there are others who do not believe in the gilded pleasure-ship at all and have steam yachts which are sturdy sea-boats and enable them to carry out cruises all over the world. Now and again one hears of a steam or motor yacht being used for a hunt after pirates' treasure, or for a scientific voyage of research into the secrets of the sea.

THE YACHT RACE

TAKING IN THE JIB-TOPSAIL

HAULING IN THE MAIN SHEET

[*Sport & General.*

YACHTS AND YACHTING

One disadvantage of the steam yacht is the stoker element. A man who is using his boat for pleasure naturally wants to keep his crew as small in number and as smart as possible, and although the average yacht hand is a very decent fellow who has mastered the art of making himself inconspicuous, the life of the stoker makes him, as a rule, a very rough man, though of course there are exceptions. And a steam yacht, unless oil-fired, means coaling, with its unpleasant noise and dirt. For this reason, and because of the much smaller

[*Sport & General.*

A HANDICAP RACE FOR YACHTS UNDER 15 TONS AT BURNHAM-ON-CROUCH

space occupied by machinery, more and more people are favouring the motor yacht, which is much cheaper to run and is nowadays as reliable as the steamer. Motor yachts can be of any size or description, from the big ocean-going ship of several hundred tons—sometimes provided with a big spread of auxiliary canvas— to the open dinghy with the little one-cylinder engine which chuffs her along splendidly and gives her owner no end of fun. A large number of life-boats are bought for conversion into motor cruisers and make very comfortable floating homes for those who prefer comfort to extravagance.

There are also, of course, the purely racing motor boats and hydro-planes, which manage an astonishing speed, lifting themselves right out of the water and dashing along in a sheet of spray, but these are for the excitement of speed only and give no other pleasure.

In addition to motor yachts, with or without auxiliary sail to help them along when the wind is fair, there are many hundreds of

[*Sport & General.*

WET TO THE SKIN AND PERFECTLY HAPPY

sailing yachts with auxiliary power, the idea being that the engine will be just big enough to kick them over a calm should they encounter one. These installations are not always satisfactory, for most yachtsmen sail when they can and therefore do not touch the engine until it is wanted in a hurry, when it is very likely to go wrong through having been neglected. The number of non-racing yachts without auxiliary power of some sort, however, is decreasing rapidly.

When one speaks of yachting most people immediately think of

[*Nautical.*

SCHOONER YACHT IN FULL SAIL

racing, although, as a matter of fact, the proportion of racing men compared with the whole body of sailing enthusiasts is comparatively small. Racing is described as a " rich man's game," and that frightens many men of moderate means who would otherwise enjoy it. Really there is no need for yachting to be at all expensive, providing a small boat is raced. A big cutter like the famous *Endeavour II*, of course, with her large paid crew, costs thousands a year, but it is doubtful if she gives as much fun as is obtained by the owners of little open boats that skim over the water with their lee gunwales awash, everybody wet to the skin and perfectly happy, with everything depending on the helmsman and his single hand.

Nowadays the tendency is all to discountenance mere money-winning races, and there are more and more class events. These classes may be international, such as the six-metre, twelve-metre and the like, where the designer has a certain amount of latitude in which he can exercise his ingenuity so long as he keeps to certain conditions, or they may be One-Design, in which case there should not be a pennyworth of difference between the boats, and success is all a matter of the skill of the helmsmen. Both kinds give excellent sport, but there are numerous other races for yachts which do not fit into any class and most of which will have been built for cruising.

Such a mixed crowd will, of course, have to be handicapped to make everything fair, and it has been found best to make a time allowance and start all off at once. Thus it may happen that the last boat to cross the line and receive her gun may, contrary to appearance, have won the race, because she has saved the time allowance she has been granted. Five minutes before the start of a race a gun is fired and all the entrants get ready, edging as close to the starting-line as they can without crossing it, for if the tip of a bowsprit is over the line when the starting gun goes, the yacht is recalled, and, keeping clear of all the others, she must manoeuvre back into position and start again.

It does not matter how one uses one's boat, whether for Society purposes, with everything elaborate and pleasant for cruises in the Mediterranean ; for knocking around the coast without care for

[*Sport & General*

RACING CLOSE-HAULED

appearances, nosing into quaint old harbours and getting the real salt of the sea; for racing against one's old competitors, or all round the coast, there is no sport in the world quite like yachting, and the doings of the Royal Naval Volunteer Supplementary Reserve during the War—at Dunkirk and elsewhere—showed of what stuff the yachtsman is made.

A CANADIAN HEAVY CARGO CARRIER

The Royal Train aboard the "Beaverdale", one of a group of ships operated by The Canadian Pacific Railway.

MOTOR BOATS

[*L. E. A.*

THE "BLUEBIRD" IN WHICH SIR MALCOLM CAMPBELL EXCEEDED A SPEED
OF 129 MILES AN HOUR AND BROKE THE WORLD'S SPEED-BOAT RECORD

[*Sport & General.*

A COASTAL MOTOR BOAT TRAVELLING AT A SPEED OF 43 KNOTS

THE CANADIAN PACIFIC LINER "EMPRESS OF CANADA" LEAVING MONTREAL

THE VOYAGE OF A CARGO LINER

JUST as the passenger expects to know when he will have to embark and when the liner in which he is sailing will arrive at his destination, so those concerned with the export and import of merchandise expect to know when their goods may be shipped and when they will be delivered.

The ships which in the main supply these needs of overseas trade are the cargo liners—those fast, modern vessels with speeds of 16 to 18 knots, which run to advertised schedules on regular routes. Such vessels frequently carry half-a-dozen passengers so let us travel with one on her voyage, say to South Africa, Australia, and back.

Having discharged her homeward cargo in London, she proceeds

[*Topical.*

A BUSY DAY AT THE ROYAL ALBERT DOCKS, LONDON
Ships unloading at the " Export Quay ". On the right is the P. & O. Liner " Chitral " undergoing
reconditioning.

to South Wales to load "railway iron," galvanised sheets, and tin-plate, and from there travels up to Birkenhead to complete her loading. Here, in addition to many thousands of pounds' worth of manufactured goods, she may load explosives and chemicals for use in the South African gold mines. Possibly, also, there may be heavy pieces for shipment, such as rolling stock for Cape Town and Durban, in the shape of coaches and Diesel-electric locomotives.

The first port of call is Cape Town, where part of the valuable

M.V. " CALEDONIAN COAST "
A modern coastal vessel of the Aberdeen Steam Navigation Co.

cargo is landed and where the ship, probably an oil-burner or motor-vessel, will re-fuel. Leaving behind Cape Town, with its famous and remarkable Table Mountain, she proceeds round the Cape to Port Elizabeth and East London, discharging cargo at both places : on again to Durban, which is probably her biggest discharging port. From Durban she travels another 300 miles up the coast to Lourenco Marques, discharging cargo for the Transvaal and the important inland city of Johannesburg : northward again

A TYPICAL BRITISH OIL-TANKER
Motor propelled and capable of carrying 15,000 tons of oil.

to Beira, with mining equipment for Bechuanaland and Nyasaland.

Now, leaving Africa, she sails round the island of Madagascar and comes to Mauritius, where she will complete the discharging

Photos]   [Nautical.

SELF-DISCHARGING COLLIER " COALHAVEN "
The hoist for raising the coal from the hold is seen in the forepart of the ship. The long arm lying amidships feeds the coal directly into barges or trucks when the boat is discharging her cargo. Derricks and cranes on the wharf are, therefore, unnecessary.

of her outward cargo by landing machinery required on the sugar plantations there.

In ballast, she proceeds right across the Indian Ocean to the Torres Strait, lying between New Guinea and the northern tip of Queensland, Australia. At Thursday Island, she pauses to pick up her pilot for the intricate passage inside the Great Barrier Reef, which stretches along the Queensland coast for over 1,200 miles in a series of coral reefs, sandy cays, and palm-covered islands. With the mainland

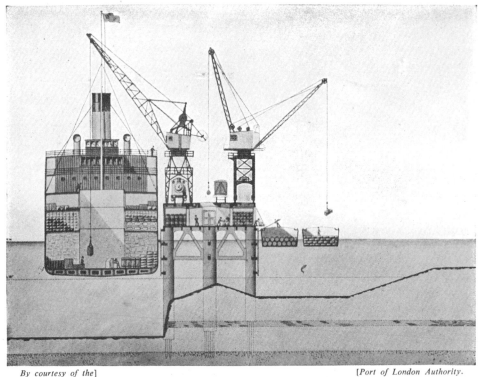

By courtesy of the]   *[Port of London Authority.*

CROSS-SECTION OF TILBURY JETTY
showing a ship's cargo being unloaded by means of cranes.

scenery to starboard it is a delightful journey, and—as fish abound—it is small wonder that the locality is very popular for fishing holidays.

The ship has certain holds fitted for the carriage of refrigerated cargo and these compartments are cleaned and cooled down before arrival at the first port, Townsville. Here, she loads first perhaps 1,500-2,000 tons of lead in " pigs ". These are stowed on the bottom of the refrigerated holds, and then completely boarded over for the loading of carcasses of frozen beef.

THE VOYAGE OF A CARGO LINER

From Townsville, she goes to Port Alma and Gladstone, loading more frozen beef and, in her ordinary cargo spaces, shipments of wool and huge casks of tallow weighing 30 cwts. apiece. Continuing on, she comes to Brisbane, loading the same type of cargo and, in addition, cases of butter and carcasses of mutton.

M.V. " CALEDONIA " (ANCHOR LINE)

After Brisbane, the ship travels on to Sydney and Melbourne, loading canned fruit and preserves, cheese and eggs (carried in " chilled " condition in 'tween-deck compartments), more frozen meat, and further bales of wool. These bales, which are of tremendous size when they come in from the ranches, are pressed or " dumped " under hydraulic presses, and are at the same time banded with hoop-iron. While they are being stowed a special cutting tool is kept handy in each compartment and when the last bale

THE S.S. " OLIVIAN COAST "
A modern vessel of the Tyne Tees Shipping Co.

175

THE VOYAGE OF A CARGO LINER

Discharging grain at Manchester Docks by means of "legs" on to electrically driven conveyor bands moving in subways beneath the quays and carrying the grain directly to a big elevator at the end of the Dock.

in a tier is in position the hoop-iron bands are cut, thus allowing the bale to expand and tighten up the whole stow.

Although if space permits a call is sometimes made at Fremantle, in Western Australia, Melbourne is generally the final loading port. Now comes the long passage to Cape Town; if it is winter time, look out for some extremely rough weather while crossing the Great Australian Bight—and more again when rounding wind-lashed Cape Agulhas and the Cape of Good Hope.

With a full cargo already on board, the Cape Town call is made purely for re-fuelling purposes. A few hours will suffice so, unless the captain and chief engineer have timed things nicely, you may not have a night in port.

The voyage schedule is nearly complete. Cape Town to the Continent and London is the last leg, and a long one. When you go ashore in London you will have travelled about 30,000 miles in five months. Glance back along the quay and you will observe that your ship is already discharging her cargo. Her next voyage dates were fixed long since and are now appearing in the shipping papers.

THE " AMERICAN RANGER " UNITED STATES LINE
(Photographed from the air.)

NEW ZEALAND REFRIGERATED SHIP

Chemical refrigeration or " Gas Storage " is practised aboard these ships, of which " Rangitata "
and " Rangitiki " are examples.

THE " SIR JAMES CLARK ROSS "

Norwegian whale factory ship, named after the famous Arctic explorer.

M.V. " ABEGWEIT " ICE-BREAKER AND CAR FERRY

This fine vessel belongs to the Canadian National Railways and transports cars and passengers across the Strait of Northumberland between New Brunswick and Prince Edward Island. She is the world's largest and most powerful ice-breaking ferry. All electric, with 8 sets of diesel engines. The Strait, nine miles across, is often frozen over.

FERRIES, ICE-BREAKERS AND RIVER STEAMERS

A TRAIN ferry between England and the Continent was talked of for many years, but it was generally thought that both the North Sea and the English Channel would be too stormy for the service to be anything but intermittent, and for that and other reasons the proposal was not pursued. The 1914-18 war, however, showed that a train service across the Channel must be established and maintained whatever the weather, and the train ferries between Richborough and France, when once started, were kept up regularly. The saving of time in the transport of war material was of the greatest importance, financially and nationally. The success of this ferry prompted the proposal to maintain a service in peace time, and this was established in the early summer of 1924, in the first instance between Harwich and Zeebrugge.

TRAIN FERRY AT SEA. " TWICKENHAM FERRY "

Now passengers can travel from Victoria Station, London, to the Gare du Nord, Paris, in under eleven hours and without moving from a luxurious bed.   This was made possible by the then Southern Railway's service of passenger-train ferries put into operation in October, 1936.   Three special train ferries were built by Messrs. Swan, Hunter & Wigham Richardson at their shipyard on the Tyne. These fine steamers, the *Shepperton Ferry* and her sisters, are 360 feet long and have a speed of 16½ knots.   They can take on board twelve sleeping cars and two baggage wagons : passengers may either

By courtesy of]   [*British Railways, Southern Region.*
CAR AND PASSENGER FERRY BETWEEN LYMINGTON AND YARMOUTH

sleep across channel, or alight from the cars and make their way to spacious public rooms, including restaurants, lounges and smoking rooms. Also, for those wishing to tour on the Continent, there is a special garage into which twenty-five motor-cars can be driven. There are four sets of rail tracks and, as an alternative to the sleeping-

By courtesy of]   *[British Railways, Southern Region.*
A VIEW OF THE TRAIN DECK ON A CROSS-CHANNEL FERRY BOAT

cars the steamers could carry forty 25-ton goods wagons. Normally, however, the two centre tracks take passenger coaches, and the outer ones take freight wagons. The value of being able to bring fragile goods from almost any part of Europe (except Russia and Spain, where the gauge is different) in one and the same wagon is obvious:

foodstuffs, such as fruit and poultry, are conveyed much more rapidly and, equally important, they are not liable to become damaged through being handled *en route*, as when they were transferred from train to ship, and then back again to train.

In order to load and unload coaches and wagons from these train ferry steamers, variations in tide levels (up to 25 feet) at Dover necessitated the building of a special train-ferry dock, the successful completion of which marked another British engineering feat.

The motorist, of course, now has his own special ferry steamers. There is the S.S. *Autocarrier*, which takes thirty-five cars and 120 passengers from Dover to Calais, and the T.S.S. *Dinard*, which carries 305 passengers and 70 to 80 cars. Also, there is the " London-Istanbul " (Dover to Ostend). This " floating garage " carries sixty cars, which are simply driven on board by means of a ramp, or inclined way.

Modern cross-channel passenger steamers are fine, fast vessels. The British Railways' T.S.S. *Falaise*, for instance, built in 1947 by Messrs. Wm. Denny & Bros., at Dumbarton, is most luxuriously

ARGENTINE RIVER STEAMER

AMERICAN RIVER BOAT

furnished. Her public rooms are air-conditioned and have fluorescent lighting. She is equipped with Radar, Radio Telephony, and a Denny-Brown stabilizer. Her speed is 20½ knots and she is on the Southampton—Channel Islands service.

Our British shipyards have built train-ferry steamers for many foreign countries, because wherever a rail service is interrupted by a river or other stretch of water too wide to be bridged the obvious solution is the train-ferry.

In America some of the larger ferry steamers take whole trains on board and carry them from one side of a river or lake to the other. The passengers can either stay in the carriages or promenade the steamer decks, as they please. In winter time, when there is much ice, the steamers have to do duty as ice-breakers as well, in order to enter or leave their slips or piers. All the latest American ferry steamers are fitted with twin screws, a pair at each end, and are double-ended, or shaped alike at the ends, so that they can proceed either end foremost. The continual agitation of the water by the numerous ferry-boats at New York and other American ports which

FERRIES, ICE-BREAKERS AND RIVER STEAMERS

BRITISH RAILWAYS TRAIN-FERRY S.S. "FALAISE" (Southern Region)
Dover—Dunkirk Service.

are subject to cold winters helps to break the ice and to prevent the water freezing. The old paddle-wheel ferry-boats were often obliged to cease running when the ice was thick, as the wheels would have been smashed by striking the floating masses.

Some of the Canadian and American ice-breaking steamers, particularly those on the northern lakes and rivers, easily make their way through ice four feet in thickness. Often they have to get through ice even thicker. At other times, on Lake Michigan and elsewhere, very rough seas are encountered by the strongly-built ferry-steamers.

In Russia and other north continental parts the " frozen winters " are extremely severe, and ice-breaking services are essential. For instance, some years ago, the captain of a British built train-ferry steamer operating in the Baltic reported having had to work his way through so much ice on one crossing that the normal four-hour journey was lengthened to 27 hours 50 minutes. Russia may be said to lead in ice-breaking, and maintains many services with ships designed for no other purpose than to keep channels and harbours clear for ordinary vessels, and for rescuing steamers which have been trapped in the ice. Some ice-breakers are fitted with a bow propeller, which is used to disturb the water and thus weaken the ice above.

All ice-breakers are built with specially strong bows, the stem being so shaped that when the vessel is steaming among ice she drives against and rises upon it and smashes through. Present-day ice-breakers can smash through a thickness of 16 ft. Very often vessels are fitted with rolling tanks in the bows, these being brought into use when the ice is very thick and does not break when the vessel rises upon it ; first one side tank is filled, then the other, causing the vessel to roll on the ice till it breaks. Ice-breakers carry, in addition to ordinary officers and crew, an ice-captain, who is an expert in the work.

The trans-Siberian Railway used to employ ice-breaking train-ferries in order to cross Lake Baikal, in Central Asia—except when the ice was solid enough to lay the rail-tracks down on it. Later, however, a connecting railway line was built round the south side of the lake.

The river steamers of America are a special type of vessel suitable for use on the great rivers, and not to be found in any other part of the world. They are fitted with accommodation that allows passengers to live as comfortably as at a first-class hotel or in a sea-going liner. They are built, too, with very shallow hulls, to enable them to pass over the many banks and shoals in the rivers ; indeed,

DANISH FRUIT CARRIER " EROS "

the story goes that one steamer needed so little water that she was able to steam over the dew on the grassy banks !

In thinking of American river steamers, the size and extent of the Great Lakes and the long, navigable rivers such as the Mississippi, the Ohio, and the Hudson, must be borne in mind. There is a tremendous volume of traffic on these rivers, and the larger steamers carry hundreds of passengers. They are capable of a very high speed,

CANADIAN PACIFIC GREAT LAKES STEAMER
" ASSINIBOIA "

although few can have beaten the record of one very old-timer, the famous *Mary Powell.* Years ago, when she was running, this steamer was once credited with having attained a speed of twenty-six miles an hour on the River Hudson. Some of these great steamers are driven by powerful screw propellers; others, again, have retained the stern paddle-wheel, or the two side paddles, which are very suitable for shallow waters. All the modern river steamers are built with a due regard to safety. They have double bottoms, watertight compartments, fire bulkheads, and a sprinkler system consisting of hundreds of outlets in all parts of the ship for extinguishing fire ; they are electrically lighted throughout, and some have a telephone in every cabin to enable a passenger to order anything he wants. They have hundreds of state-rooms, and every possible convenience in the way of lounges, restaurants, smoking-rooms, and so on, for their many passengers.

FERRIES, ICE-BREAKERS AND RIVER STEAMERS

It has already been mentioned that paddle-wheels are particularly suitable to shallow waters; this is because of the " snags " or under-water obstructions likely to damage a screw propeller, which must be much deeper in the water to be effective. Side-wheelers and stern paddle steamers are still used in several other parts.

Suitable though the paddle-steamer is for shallow waters, an ingenious method of adapting the screw to those waters is that of placing it in a tunnel or tube, open at both ends, partly above the water line; when the screw revolves it fills the tunnel or tube with water, and is thus as effective as though it were submerged in the ordinary way.

On the great rivers of India and Burma, such as the Ganges, Bhramaputra, and Irrawaddy, very large river steamers are used to carry produce and passengers. Steamers of special design are also used to navigate the wonderful gorges on the Upper Yangtze, where there are tremendous whirlpools and eddies.

[L. N. A.

A " WHALEBACK " STEAMER IN THE SAULT ST. MARIE CANAL AFTER A COLD TRIP ON LAKE SUPERIOR. SHE WAS COATED WITH 20 INCHES OF ICE

THE " AQUITANIA " (CUNARD WHITE STAR LINE), 45,647 TONS

Length 902 feet, breadth 97 feet. Light M.A.... 56 feet 4 inches 6 to 11½

UNLOADING FLOUR AT THE ROYAL VICTORIA DOCKS   [*Fox Photos.*

STOWING AN OUTWARD CARGO

EVERYONE knows about the export drive and the need for producing more and more goods for sale abroad, and everyone knows that we must do this in order to pay for our necessary imports of foodstuffs and raw materials. So, when the goods have been manufactured, down they go to the docks to be loaded and stowed in our outward bound cargo liners.

If, in any of our big seaports, you have watched a stream of lorries converging on this or that particular gateway to dockland, you may well have wondered how such a bewildering assortment of manufactures is dealt with in one ship. Piled high on the lorries, you may note such diverse items as bales of cotton goods, sheets of asbestos roofing, cases of machinery, bundles and bars of steel, drums of paint and oil, awkward and heavy castings, cases of beer and cigarettes, and scores of other commodities. It is the stevedore's complicated job to load all these products of factory and workshop into the ship.

The assortment of goods, however, is only part of the problem of loading a general cargo. Watch any particular queue of lorries closely enough and you will see that the goods being carried are not all stencilled, or " port-marked," for the same destination. One lorry-load may be of goods marked for Penang ; the next one may be for Port Swettenham ; the third, fourth, and fifth may be for Singapore, Hong Kong, and Shanghai. If you glance along the line of slowly moving vehicles these port names will be seen to be recurring over and over again. This is because very few cargo vessels load only for one destination. Whatever trade they are in, they generally load for a sequence of ports along their route.

TESTING A " JUMBO " DERRICK
50 tons of concrete blocks being lifted.

In other words, the initial problem of stowing iron and steel and heavy chemical products on the bottom of the ship where they will not crush, damage, or taint more fragile goods is multiplied by the number of ports for which the vessel loads. Moreover, it must be remembered that, as the ship comes to each successive port, so the stevedores in those places must be able to discharge all the goods intended for their destination. For instance, if the order of the ports is Penang, Port Swettenham, Singapore, Hong Kong, and Shanghai, then all the Penang cargo must be available at once and not " over-stowed " by cargo for any of the other ports—and so with the rest of the cargo until the ship leaves Hong Kong for Shanghai.

But before ever those goods arrive at the docks for shipment, a number of necessary matters will have been settled. First, the shipping company will have advertised their vessel as sailing for the various stated ports on such and such a date ; their outward freight department will then receive numerous enquiries from shippers (people and firms who export goods) and will gradually " book " their cargo to the capacity of the ship. Certain special items and all awkward and heavy packages are referred to their stevedore to make sure they can be accommodated. Then, in consultation with their stevedore and wharfinger, delivery dates are arranged and the ship's cargo begins to flow towards the loading berth.

The stevedore is the man who plans and controls the loading and stowage of the ship ; the wharfinger is the man whose staff receive the cargo into the sheds, checking the loads and the weights and measurements of the packages—because it is according to the weight and measurement of their cargo that shippers pay their freight.

There are, of course, a lot of commodities which may arrive by train or barge. Big shipments of steel are generally sent to the dock by rail, and chemicals from the Imperial Chemical Industries usually arrive by barge and are loaded from overside. First into the ship we are loading will be all available iron and steel for Shanghai, and the heavy chemicals like soda-ash and caustic soda. These last are always stowed " on their own ground " as their corrosive nature may damage even steelwork. Some of the iron and steel may be bundles and bars up to 40 feet in length, and sometimes longer ; or there may be a shipment of bridge material or steelwork for erecting a works or factory on the banks

LOADING UP
A 43-ton diesel locomotive being hauled aboard.

of the Yangtse river. Such constructional steel is sometimes prefabricated into massive box girders weighing six or more tons. To load these, the stevedores must bear in mind the Safe Working Load of the ship's derricks and of the wires to be used in hoisting the girders from quay to ship. No gear in use must ever be overloaded or an accident may occur and someone be killed or injured. For really heavy packages the ship's heavy, or " jumbo," derrick will have to be used, and with this massive derrick and its four or five-fold gear in use pieces of machinery up to 50 tons may be handled. Some

189

vessels have heavy derricks capable of handling 100-120 tons, but a 50-ton " jumbo " is more general, and pieces over this weight are loaded by floating crane—always assuming that at the port of destination there is similar facility for discharge.

When such heavy packages have been lowered into the ship's hold there arises the problem of their stowage. The stevedore will try to arrange for them to be placed in the centre of the compartment, filling the ends and sides with handier cargo, but this cannot always be managed. In cases where heavy packages must be stowed in one end of a compartment, the men in the hold rig up a system of pulleys which they attach to the package and also to one or two of a number of ringbolts built into the ship's structure. Using the ship's winches, they gradually heave the package into the required stowage position.

A most important export is that of textile goods, covering a wide range of woollen and cotton cloth for suits, dresses, shirts and so on. These goods are packed in bales and cases and are known as " fine goods." They are given careful stowage where they cannot be damaged by other cargo or rain. Any cargo liable to be damaged by rain is kept under cover in the ends of the holds, leaving the open " square of the hatch " for " rough " cargo.

Another notable export to-day, which calls for special planning by the stevedore, is that of uncased motor-cars which are shipped virtually ready-for-the-road. These are frequently driven to the docks from Coventry, Birmingham and elsewhere, and only their batteries, petrol and oil are removed. Sometimes, one hundred or more are shipped in one vessel. Obviously, they must have " top stowage " and the ideal position is in the shallow 'tween-deck compartments of the ship rather than in the lower holds. But, very frequently, these 'tween-decks cannot be spared. They are wanted for all manner of " special stowage " cargoes which will be mentioned later. The stevedore sighs, and decides that he will have to give the motor-cars lower hold stowage after all. This is arranged by building up the lower holds with ordinary general cargo until within 6 feet of the top. At this height a level is made for the cars. Possibly several lower holds have to be so arranged, and it is amazing how a good holdsman can, with cases and bales and packages of varying dimensions, nevertheless so stow them as to create this level platform. Dunnage wood, consisting of flat boards, is then placed over the cargo. The cars are hoisted on board by special slings, or by a frame which touches only the rubber tyres, and wheeled and steered into position in their floating garage. Carpenters next secure them with timber-work extending around the wheels and, finally, dust sheets cover their shining splendour for the voyage.

Coming up into the 'tween-decks, there are all the "special stowage" commodities to be dealt with. First may be mentioned perhaps several hundred tons of paint, oil, distemper, dyes, and other liquid and paste cargoes in drums which, of course, must never be placed on top of ordinary general cargo on account of possible leakage. There will also be shipments of asbestos sheets, some flat and some corrugated. These are stowed on a bed of sawdust and stacked to the height of the deck, care being taken that the edges of the sheets are not chipped during handling. Other "special stowage" items are drums or packages whose contents may be harmful to certain other goods. For instance, there are to-day many chemical products which must not be stowed adjacent to foodstuffs—

[Fox Photos.

S.S. "ANCHISES" (BLUE FUNNEL LINER)
Unloading barrels of coconut oil at King George V. Docks, London.

others which are inflammable and must be stowed away from acids or commodities liable to spontaneous combustion. Cylinders containing various liquid or permanent gases must be stowed not less than 8 feet from the side of the ship—a precaution taken in case of collision, when the cylinders might be subject to great shock and burst.

In one of the 'tween decks most ships have a " strong-room," or special compartment partitioned off by a steel bulkhead. It is kept under lock and key and *ad valorem* cargo is stowed here. This is cargo of especial value upon which extra freight has been paid. When possible, cases of whisky are given strong-room stowage, as are shipments of banknotes, and if space permits after all the valuables have been stowed, mail also is placed there. The strong-room is opened only by one of the ship's officers.

Sometimes there are items of awkward cargo which are too large to go into any of the ship's holds. These are instead frequently carried on the vessel's upper deck. Huge locomotives, launches, tugboats, exceptionally big pieces of constructional steelwork are examples of such deck cargoes. When these are loaded, special precautions are taken in lashing and securing them against bad weather conditions and heavy rolling. Other deck cargoes carried include such widely differing items as race-horses and other animals, and cargoes which may not be carried below decks on account of their dangerous nature.

All the time loading is taking place, a " plan-maker " is busy building up a complete plan of the stowage. The final copies are coloured according to the various ports, and this important document provides the ship's officers and the stevedores abroad with a reliable guide as to how and where the cargo is stowed.

Another document handed to the chief officer gives the distribution of weight. Suppose that for Penang the total weight of cargo on board is 800 tons ; this document details how this 800 tons is distributed—150 tons in Number One hatch, 200 tons in Number Two, and so on. Each successive port is dealt with separately, and the document is very necessary in assessing the length of time the ship is likely to take discharging her various hatches at each port.

Along with other documentation, the wharfinger's staff provide the outward freight department with the information necessary to compile the ship's manifest—a document of many sheets listing every package of cargo on board, by whom it is shipped and to whom.

H.M.S. " CONWAY "

The famous Cadet School ship now stationed in the Menai Straits. Hundreds of officers in the Royal Navy and the Mercantile Marine are " old Conway boys." The vessel was once the battleship " Nile."

THE MAKING OF A SAILOR

IT would be a disastrous day for England if boys ceased to wish to become sailors.   Think of the pictures of all the fine ships in this book, and then try to imagine them idle and laid up in the docks for want of officers and men to run them.   Besides, what would happen ? Quite apart from the hundreds of thousands of people unable to travel for business or pleasure, how would the inhabitants of this country live without the food and material brought in day after day by all these vessels ?   Fortunately, such a state of affairs is well nigh impossible.   We have seafaring in our blood, and it is safe to say that there will always be boys whose thoughts turn early to " a life on the ocean wave."   Some boys will think of the Royal Navy ; others will have their imagination stirred by thoughts of visiting far-off countries, of carrying passengers and cargo across the seven seas, and of becoming officers and finally captains of the ships of our Merchant Navy.

For the boy who feels this desire for a seafaring career, the very first and wisest step is to undergo an eyesight test.   Good vision is absolutely essential, and no boy who is colour-blind can ever become a navigating officer.   There are Mercantile Marine Offices in most British ports, where your eyes may be tested for a very small fee.

Also, it is wise to have them examined by an eye-specialist because while you may at the time be able to read the Ministry of Transport's letter and number tests at the required distances, and to distinguish the red, green, and white lights in the dark-room, there may be some eye weakness which might develop later. The visit to the eye-specialist is much more preferable than the awful discovery that, after several years as an apprentice, your eyes are beginning to fail and you must leave the sea.

You have decided on the Merchant Navy, and your eyes are sound and up to the required standard. What is the next step in the making of a sailor ? It is to determine whether you wish to go straight to sea and serve four years' apprenticeship in a liner or cargo vessel, or whether—in preparation for this—you would prefer to have two years' training in H.M.S. *Conway*, moored off Bangor, in the Menai Strait ; or at the Thames Nautical Training College, Greenhithe, Kent ; or again two or three years at Messrs. Devitt and Moore's shore training establishment, the Nautical College, Pangbourne, Berkshire. Such previous training will count as one year's sea apprenticeship, and will cost between £150 and £200 a year in fees. There is also the School of Navigation, University College, Southampton, where you may take a 40 weeks' course, counting as 6 months' sea apprenticeship.

On board the training ship, or at the shore establishments, you rank as a cadet and wear the appropriate blue uniform. The usual age for entry is somewhere between thirteen and fifteen, and, in addition to continuing your ordinary general education, you are taught all nautical subjects by Royal Naval and Royal Naval Reserve officers and instructors. Thus a boy who has worked properly, leaves training ship or college knowing many things about the sea and ships and their navigation ; and with knowledge of seamanship and boat-handling. A number of the big shipping companies take the greatest interest in these training establishments and often prefer to take as apprentices, boys who have been to one of them. Therefore, for those who can afford it, such preparation is an advantage.

Previous training, however, is not essential and many boys go direct to sea from their ordinary schools. Others again, take the short course available at the Outward Bound Sea School, Aberdovey, sponsored by a well-known shipping company. Here, boys from all walks of life learn how to mix, and with the emphasis upon their

MANNING THE MAST AT A TRAINING SCHOOL

SEAMANSHIP CLASS, PANGBOURNE COLLEGE

physical fitness, are generally "shown the ropes" in readiness for sea.

It must not be thought that the training establishments first mentioned are the only ones in existence. They have been named first because they are the ones which specialize in the training of officers. There is the *Mercury*, on the River Hamble below Southampton, but training here is not specialized for the officer class only, and technical training for Wireless Operator, Electrician, Artificer, and the lower deck is given. There are many others which specialize more in the training of boys to be Able Seamen, Stewards, and Stokers, such as the *Arethusa*, the *Indefatigable*—now a shore-based school— and many other establishments in or near big seaports. Although all of these train boys mostly for other than officer rank and are much less expensive than the ones first mentioned, it must not be supposed that a boy going to sea from one of them cannot become an officer. Many well-known commanders of ships began life as deck-boys. Generally speaking, for a boy who wishes to enter later some special Service or Pilotage, training on the *Conway*, at Pangbourne or at the Thames Nautical Training College, will be found very advantageous, and these establishments nominate regularly a certain number of midshipmen for the Royal Navy and the Royal Naval Reserve. Facilities and details for entering any training ship or shore establishment will be furnished by the Ministry of Transport Superintendent at any Mercantile Marine Office, who will also be pleased to give advice on the question of apprenticeship to shipping companies.

Many companies have now discontinued their former practice of requiring premiums on apprenticeship, while in other cases modifications have been made. Sometimes the apprentice is paid a small wage and perhaps a bonus sum at the conclusion of his training. This bonus scheme is very helpful to a young man of twenty who must take up residence in some seaport while preparing for examination for his Second Mate's Certificate.

As a first voyage apprentice, a boy goes through the usual mill of inexperience, and it depends upon himself how he pulls through. The young apprentice straight from an inland home who takes amiss the practical jests of shipmates, makes a big mistake. They should be taken in the right spirit ; one day, the youngster will himself be the

COMPASS AND CHART WORK ON THE TERRACE, PANGBOURNE COLLEGE

PHYSICAL EXERCISES, PANGBOURNE COLLEGE

jester. Some of the jokes played are rather amusing. A shipmate will rush up to the first-voyager and say, " Quick ! the officer of the watch wants some green oil for the starboard light." The apprentice sets out in his quest for " green oil." He asks various shipmates, and wonders when they smile and direct him hither and thither. Finally he goes to the officer and confesses failure. The officer may be busy and reply brusquely that there is no green oil for the starboard light, which shows green because of the coloured shade in the lamp. Or he may look at the apprentice with twinkling eyes and remember his own first voyage. In this case, he may say, " Never mind the green oil, sonny. Go and ask the second engineer for ' the key of the keelson ! ' " Down goes the youngster, to face a Scotsman, perhaps, with red, glistening face, who looks away with a smile

THE BAND, PANGBOURNE COLLEGE

and watches the cranks of great reciprocating engines flying round, or glances at pressure-gauges and listens to the steady hum of the turbines, or the phut-phut of Diesels. There is, of course, no " key of the keelson " and the fruitless search may go on for an hour. It sounds silly perhaps, but it is all part of the changing of a " landlubber " into a sailor. During the search, the youngster will be directed to all manner of strange places in the ship, and will thus learn at once the whereabouts of " the bos'n's locker," " the fore-peak," " the fiddley," and so on.

BOAT PRACTICE, PANGBOURNE COLLEGE

These early first-voyage days soon pass, and the apprentice gradually settles down to his new life in the " half-deck," the name given to the apprentices' room, which is usually one of the midship deck-houses. It is separate from the seamen's fo'c'sle, and separate also from the officer's saloon accommodation—although in most companies, apprentices take their meals with the officers.

In a week or so he will have learned how to climb masts, how never to fling the dirty water from a scrubbing bucket to windward instead of to leeward. (He may do this once but, if the chief officer sees him and takes one glance at the spoiled paintwork, he will certainly never do it again !) He will learn also how to balance himself on a heaving deck. One word about seasickness. Do not imagine that the captain or officers are unduly hard-hearted if they keep seasick first-voyagers at work, because this is one of the finest cures for overcoming the malady once and for all.

Methods of training vary with different companies, but in the good cargo vessel type of ship, apprentices have opportunity to learn something of everything about their future profession. They start, perhaps, on day work and are called at 5.30 a.m., ready to work with the seamen. Sometimes, it is claimed that intending officers should not be made to work with the sailors—painting, "holystoning" decks, cleaning out holds, and so on. But such talk is nonsense. How can the chief officer of a ship tell the bos'n and his men what to do and how to do it, better than from his own personal experience ?

THE TRAINING SHIP "ARETHUSA,"
moored in the Thames at Greenhithe, Kent. The old 50-gun frigate is of interest as having been the last British man-of-war to go into action entirely under sail (Odessa, 1854).

On the other hand, such work can be overdone, and when selecting a shipping company it is important to send a boy only to a good company, where he will receive proper instruction in all future duties.

Besides practical seamanlike work, which will include the splicing of wire and rope, the mixing of paint, the lowering and raising of derricks, the handling of winches and boats, and all their gear, the apprentices take watches at times with the officers. Up on the bridge they learn how the actual navigation is done, how the ship's position is plotted on the chart, how the entries are made in the log-book, how the barometer is used to forecast the weather, and a dozen other things. They are taught how to use a sextant, and how to take sun and star observations with it.

THE MAKING OF A SAILOR

At other times, they may take a few watches with the engineer, and learn some first principles of ship machinery. When entering and leaving port, they will be stationed with an officer, and will learn how ships are manœuvred into dock, and how made fast, or anchored. In port, they will work under the supervision of an officer, and learn how to stow and discharge cargo. They will learn only the beginnings of such matters, because years of experience go to the making of a successful officer, who knows instinctively that tea and

THE " ARETHUSA "
March Past of boys, headed by the band.

tobacco must be stowed well away from copra or other heating cargo, and that many fruits will taint not only other cargo but each other.

When apprenticeship is complete—that is, after four years at sea, or three years if previously at a ship or shore training establishment—the young man now comes ashore and usually spends a few weeks in preparation for his first examination, which he will sit for when he is about twenty years of age. The examination takes some days, and covers all the nautical subjects in which training should have been given. These include navigation, seamanship, chart work, elementary engineering knowledge, and signals. Also, he must obtain a lifeboat certificate, and another for rendering first-aid.

SIGNALLING CLASS, PANGBOURNE COLLEGE

Having satisfied the Ministry of Transport examiners and obtained his Second Mate's Certificate, he is qualified to go to sea as an officer. But only in a tramp steamer, and then very seldom, is he likely to obtain a second officer's post. In bigger ships he may be third or fourth officer, and in liners possibly seventh or eighth officer. After eighteen months' service he is eligible to sit for his First Mate's Certificate, and after another eighteen months as an officer afloat he can sit for "Master." Naturally, both these examinations are more difficult than the first one. Later still, really ambitious young men will sit for "Extra Master." This certificate is not actually necessary because "Master" qualifies an officer to command a ship, but it is sometimes essential for certain specialized posts connected with the sea and ships.

As in other professions, the end of examinations is not the end of learning. The sea itself, with its ever-

INSTRUCTION UNDER SAIL: ON THE BRIG

THE MAKING OF A SAILOR

changing moods, provides a life-long study for the man who would be a successful shipmaster, and wishes to come to the end of his career with a fine, clean record of service in the Merchant Navy.

To become a qualified engineer on a sea-going steamer is a long and somewhat arduous process. A boy should begin by serving an apprenticeship in an engineering workshop, if possible one in which marine work is done, for four or five years, to secure the workshop qualification for examination for an engineer's certificate of competency. After this workshop time he must put in eighteen months at sea on regular watch on the main engines or boilers, and if his workshop service, or the equivalent which is allowed, complies with the Ministry of Transport regulations, he may sit for his examination for a second-class certificate, and afterwards put in another eighteen months' sea service before he sits for his first-class certificate. Intending engineers should buy a copy of *Regulations relating to the Examination of Engineers in the Mercantile Marine*, in which they will find all the information required.

THE MARINER'S COMPASS

The card by which the vessel is steered is so constructed that it always remains level, no matter how violent the motion of the ship ; its face bears a circle marked with 32 points, equidistant, and sometimes each space between the points is divided into half points and quarter points. Beginning with North, the next is North a quarter east, North a half east, and so on. To recite all the points correctly and give their opposites is called "boxing the compass." The needle always points to the North, though there is a variation in different parts of the world between the magnetic pole and the geographical pole that sailors have to learn to allow for.

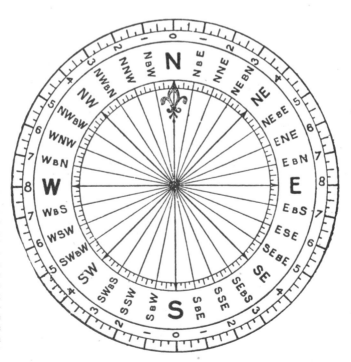

The huge bow port, about 18 feet in diameter, is closed by a great lid operated by a girder arm. Through this port the whales are hauled bodily up a steel ramp to the weather deck, where they are cut up.

THE " ATHENIC " TWIN-SCREW OIL-BURNING TURBINE STEAMER (15,187 TONS)
Shaw Savill line

A DAY IN THE LIFE OF A LINER OFFICER

PERHAPS you have often thought you would like to be an officer of a stately liner when you grow up. This little article is an attempt to describe a typical day in the life of the Second Officer of a large ship at sea. You will gather that the post, like all positions worth holding, requires a great deal of knowledge and close attention to work, and that there is a lot to be done apart from walking the deck resplendent in gold lace.

The Second Officer is called fifteen minutes before midnight by a quartermaster—who is wisely ordered to return a few minutes before twelve o'clock to make *quite* sure that his first visit was effective ! A minute or so after eight bells the officer proceeds to the bridge, which on a dark, cold and stormy night offers, as you can well imagine, an unpleasant contrast to a cosy bunk in a nice warm cabin. He is usually received with considerable welcome by the Third Officer. He is to relieve the " Third," who hands over the ship to him, giving particulars as to the course, her speed, and the reading of the patent log at midnight. He also informs him if the portholes are open, as, in the event of stormy weather, the order will have to be given to have them closed, so that sleeping passengers may not be rudely awakened by a " green sea " washing them out of their bunks. He also points out any ships that may be in sight and any other lights that are visible. The Third Officer usually talks for a few minutes until the " Second " " gets his eyes," or in other words has become accustomed to the darkness. The " Third " then goes below with a somewhat jubilant demeanour which the " Second " rarely finds agreeable. A steward usually brings a nice cup of tea and sandwiches to the bridge. The long vigil begins and the officer " walks the bridge " almost like a soldier on sentry-go. As he passes the compass, he glances at the card to make sure that the ship is being accurately steered, which is, of course, of the utmost importance. Every time he walks to the starboard side he looks with particular care in that direction, as his ship must, under the Rule of the Road, give way to other vessels crossing from that side.

[*Central Press.*

A HIGHLY PRIVILEGED PASSENGER HAS A CHAT WITH THE CAPTAIN

Every half-hour the bell strikes the time and every hour the quartermaster reports the reading of the patent log. About 2 a.m. when time appears to pass very slowly, a cup of tea arrives from below. The middle watch, as the Second Officer's watch is called, is sometimes referred to as the " Grave-yard Watch "—possibly because it embraces the darkest and most silent hours of the night.

It is a wonderful experience to be one of the few who are awake in a floating city of perhaps a thousand souls, and to have the lives of

[*Topical.*

FOR PRACTICE ONLY

The starboard boats of the "Aquitania" being launched after an order to "Abandon Ship." Such drill is of great service in rendering the officers and crew familiar with their duties in case of disaster. In the "Aquitania" and other large vessels passengers have their boat stations marked out in their cabins, and all they have to do is to follow the arrow which directs them to their boat.

CLEANING A FUNNEL TOP ON ONE OF THE GIANT CUNARDERS

all these people in your hands ; one of the greatest compensations for the many drawbacks of a life at sea is that feeling of responsibility, most marked, perhaps, during the dark and silent hours of the middle watch. During each watch the officer, whenever possible, takes an observation of some star which will enable him to check an error of the compass, which is changing constantly throughout the voyage.

If the weather should become foggy, or hard rain set in, the officer, according to regulations, causes the steam whistle to be blown ; this usually disturbs all but the heaviest sleepers and sometimes alarms passengers, but it must be done. The writer learned the importance of the rule when he was first in charge of a watch as a very junior officer. The ship—a cargo vessel —was sailing from Mauritius to Colombo, a route rarely used. One night the ship passed through a tropical rain squall so heavy that one could hardly see at all ; the officer sounded the whistle frequently, until a passenger, an " old and crochety gentleman," called up from below that he could not get a wink of sleep for the noise. The officer was framing a suitable reply when, out of the driving rain, appeared a steamer's lights. She was right ahead and steaming directly for us on an opposite course. We altered " hard a-starboard " immediately; the other ship acted likewise, and we escaped a collision by what seemed to be a few feet. That experience taught one that the *least* possible *may* happen at sea.

THE S.S. "WASHINGTON" (UNITED STATES LINES).

Reproduced from the painting by Worden Wood.

A DAY IN THE LIFE OF A LINER OFFICER

The Chief Officer is called at 3.45, and appears on the bridge at 4. The Second Officer then hands the ship over to the "Chief" in the same way that it was handed over to him. He writes out the log book —a diary of all that has happened during the watch

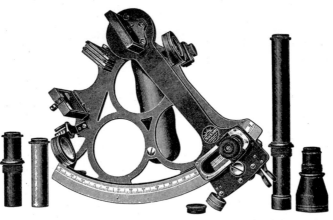

By courtesy of]   [H. Hughes & Sons, Ltd.

A SEXTANT

A sextant, as its name implies, is approximately the sixth part of a circle. The instrument enables navigating officers to measure the altitude of the celestial bodies and other angular distances.

—and then goes down to his cabin. He is usually fast asleep in a few minutes, to be called again at about 7.30 when he takes his bath and dresses, so as to be in time to be in the chart-room at 8 o'clock. Here he winds the chronometers and has to make a special report of having carried out that important duty to the Captain. Many second officers give orders that a card be placed on their plate at breakfast as a reminder in case they forget. Shortly after 8 o'clock, along with most of the other officers, he takes the "morning sight" of the sun, which enables him to find the approximate position of the ship, which is confirmed or corrected at noon. The Second Officer, who is usually the navigating officer, alters the ship's clocks accordingly; often all the clocks of the ship are controlled by the "master clock" in the chart room. After this he goes down to breakfast, and the passengers at his table probably "rag" him jokingly for disturbing them during the night by sounding the steam whistle. After breakfast, he may read for awhile, and will then perhaps work on "mail books," as he is in charge of the mails, a duty which entails a

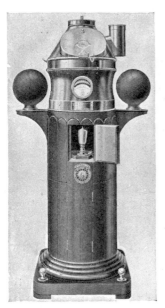

THE "KELVITE" STANDARD COMPASS

The compass card is lighted from below by means of the electric lamp enclosed in the binnacle.

great deal of clerical work. Perhaps he may superintend the cleaning and overhauling of the various important navigational instruments which are in his care. During the forenoon he will probably take part in some deck-games with the passengers, or " yarn " with the Chief Officer, who is also on " watch below." The quartermaster informs him when it is 11.45, and he goes on to the bridge to take

" LADY RODNEY " FLAGSHIP OF THE CANADIAN NATIONAL STEAMSHIPS WEST INDIES FLEET

sights at noon, when the ship's position is found by observation of the sun. He then takes over the watch again from the Third Officer, being relieved for half an hour at 1 p.m. for lunch. At 3.30 he usually takes " sights " again for longitude, and at 4 p.m. is relieved by the Chief Officer.

For some reason or other you will find that the Second Officer usually has a large number of friends among the juvenile passengers,

THE " FRANCONIA " (CUNARD WHITE STAR LINE), 20,158 TONS

A good example of a popular type of Atlantic liner, of fairly moderate dimensions, but providing all the comforts of the larger vessels. The sports arena extends through two decks, and has an area of 6,000 feet, with swimming bath, gymnasium and squash rackets court. There is also a clear space for all kinds of deck-games.

A DAY IN THE LIFE OF A LINER OFFICER

VANCOUVER, BRITISH COLUMBIA

and it is a common thing for him to find four or five young guests awaiting him in his cabin when he arrives from the bridge at 4 p.m. These tea parties are very cheerful occasions and are often attended by the Third Officer.

From 6 to 8 is called the " Second Dog Watch "—and in the old sailing-ship days was a time for recreation among the ship's company. This spirit still lives and is felt in the life of an officer on board a modern passenger liner. At 6.30 the first bugle is usually sounded, and the officer changes in readiness for dinner at 7. After dinner there may be a concert or a dance, from which the Second Officer, often very reluctantly, retires about 8.30 at which early hour he goes to bed and sleeps soundly, that he may be ready to take over the middle watch again at midnight.

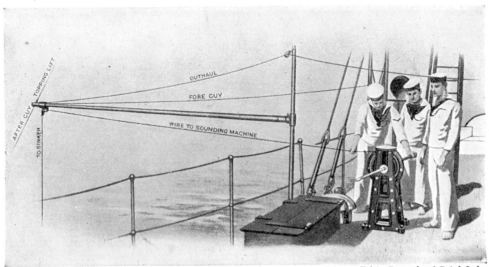

By courtesy of]   *[Messrs. Kelvin, Bottomley & Baird, Ltd.*
TAKING SOUNDINGS FROM THE NAVIGATING BRIDGE BY MEANS OF LORD KELVIN'S SOUNDING MACHINE
The installation of this apparatus on the bridge enables the navigating officer himself to read the depth of each cast instead of being dependent on a message conveyed from aft.

THE MOTOR VESSEL "PORT BRISBANE" PORT LINE (12,000 tons)
Note the attractive squat funnel of unusual design.

S.S. "STRATHAIRD" (22,500 TONS) P. & O. & BRITISH INDIA COMPANY
Reconditioned with only one funnel instead of three.

IRISH CROSS-CHANNEL STEAMER " LEINSTER "

A TYPICAL BRITISH BUCKET DREDGER

By courtesy of]
A GRIMSBY TRAWLER
[Smith's Dock Co., Ltd.

THE SHIPS YOU SEE WHEN ON HOLIDAY

NO matter where you go by the seaside in Great Britain there are nearly always ships of some sort to be seen, and distinguishing the various types is one of the most fascinating occupations of a holiday. It is, moreover, exceedingly simple once you have grasped a few general principles. The most primitive type, of course, is the *Lighter*, which is just a floating box for the carriage of cargo, without power of its own. It is to be seen drifting down the current of a river or being towed. Lighters form a valuable means of loading cargo from overside, thus relieving the congestion of crowded quays. Similarly, cargo discharged into them is often taken direct to a riverside warehouse.

The *Sailing Barge* can always be distinguished at once because its mainsail, generally of heavy red canvas, is supported by a huge sprit boom which goes from corner to corner and is always standing. These barges are very economical, because they can be handled by two or three men on quite long voyages, and, having flat bottoms,

BECALMED OFF THE START
From the picture by Maurice Randall

can rest anywhere. In the open sea, however, they have the disadvantage that, in rolling, the heavy boom is apt to smash things, and until shortly before the war, sea voyages for which a flat bottom was required were usually undertaken by *Ketches*. These little boats, generally more shapely than a barge and with one tall and one short mast, are, however, now rapidly disappearing from use. Indeed, steam and motor driven craft are ousting all sailing types and out of 3,000 sailing barges in commission some 15 years ago only 300 now remain.

The more ambitiuos rigs than the barge or ketch are even less

[*Nautical.*

THAMES RACING BARGE UNDER FULL SAIL

in evidence today. Within certain limits the sailing coaster contrived to do wonders, but beyond them the wind and tide had a greatly increased influence, and when a merchant was " ordering short," relying on delivery within a few days, he was very apt to be let down and would insist on his goods being delivered by a ship with power which could keep a reasonable time-table.

The only other sailing ships besides these types and purely pleasure craft that one is likely to see round the coast are such *Fishing Smacks* as are left. They are now generally fitted with auxiliary motors to help them to drag their trawls along the bottom of the sea. It is always easy to tell a fishing boat from any other

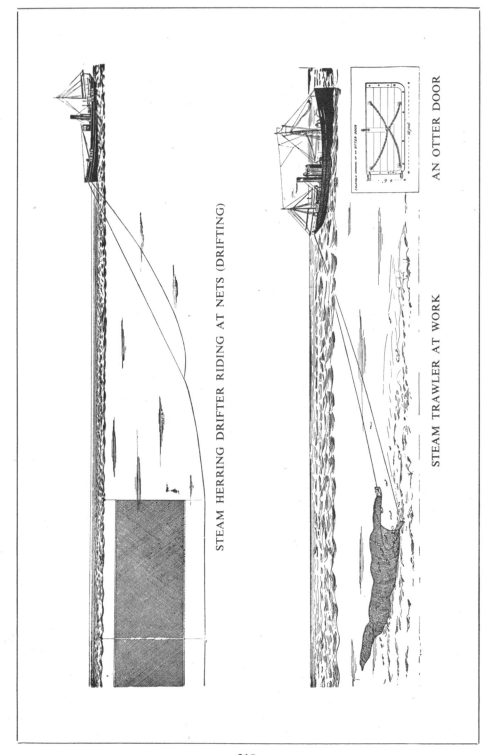

STEAM HERRING DRIFTER RIDING AT NETS (DRIFTING)

STEAM TRAWLER AT WORK

AN OTTER DOOR

because it is bound by law to have a number painted in huge figures on the hull, prefixed by a letter, or letters, standing for the port at which it is registered. Thus R. for Ramsgate, Gy. for Grimsby, etc. This law applies to foreign fishing boats as well as to British and enables them to be easily identified should they be breaking any of the many fishing laws, or engaged in smuggling, as so many of them were in olden days. Most motor fishing vessels carry a fair spread of canvas to help their engines when there is any sort of a breeze, but the majority of British fishing craft are steam, either trawlers or drifters. The *Trawler* is the bigger type and drags its

Photo]

A DRIFTER ADAPTED FOR TRAWLING

[*Nautical*.

net along the bottom of the sea ; the smaller *Drifter* is distinguishable by having her foremast hinged so that it drops down and lies alongside the funnel when she has her nets spread on either side of her and held on the top of the water to catch surface fish like herring and mackerel. In many small ports, however, there is not enough water for the normal type of trawler, and there are not enough surface fish to attract the drifters, so the fishermen take an ordinary drifter hull and fit it with trawling gear, sometimes rather a dangerous experiment. Trawlers and drifters are much the same all over the country, but sailing and motor craft vary locally in many respects so that it is easy for a sailor to say at once where she hails from.

THE SHIPS YOU SEE WHEN ON HOLIDAY

After the various types of fishing craft, perhaps the most common vessel to be seen round the coast is the *Tug*, which can always be distinguished by her appearance of being pushed up forward. She is so designed to get the big towing hook as near the middle of the ship as possible, and abaft this hook the deck is spanned by heavy wooden towing rails which prevent the rope from catching on to anything and probably carrying it away. All tugs have a characteristic low stern, on which the bulwarks slope inward, the reason for this being that if they were of ordinary pattern the tow rope would speedily wrench them away as the tug pitches in a sea. Some tugs, especially paddlers, are used during the summer months to carry passengers.

ELDER DEMPSTER MOTOR VESSEL " SHERBRO "

To describe all the various types of *Cargo Steamers* that one sees would be a long task, but it is not difficult to distinguish the principal classes. A great amount of cargo is carried up and down the coast in small steamers and motor ships, often hard to distinguish from steam trawlers except for the absence of the big white numbers on their bows. In most of these vessels the funnel is well aft, in order to give a clear hold for the carriage of cargo, as it is much quicker and more convenient to unload from one length of the ship than from widely separated spaces. The *Motor Coasters* often seen on the coast have no funnel at all, and sometimes just a small pipe, while others have quite a stout smoke stack, as big as that of an average steamer ; this carries their exhaust, and sometimes also the smoke from the boiler which many possess for working the winches which handle their cargo. Motor vessels can generally be distinguished from steamers by the colour of the smoke that comes from this

M.V. "WINCHESTER". SOUTHERN RAILWAY CARGO BOAT. SOUTHAMPTON
TO THE CHANNEL ISLANDS.

funnel or by the virtual absence of smoke—because there is sometimes
only a very slight haze to be seen coming from the funnel of a vessel
driven by Diesel engines.

Overseas Cargo Steamers and *Motor Vessels* are of all types,
mostly with one funnel between two masts, and it requires a great
deal of experience to distinguish the different lines and to say just
where each vessel is going. At some of the ports where they trade
shore cranes are not available and for this reason most vessels have

BRITISH PADDLE STEAMER "LINCOLN CASTLE"

THE " ROYAL EAGLE," GENERAL STEAM NAVIGATION CO.

a number of upright sampson posts to support the derricks which handle their cargoes. These sampson posts are generally used as ventilators as well.

Passenger Liners nearly always have a big cargo capacity as well as their cabins, and therefore will often possess a number of these sampson posts, but such passenger vessels can generally be distinguished by their added passenger decks, and by the long row of life-boats along either side compared with the two, four, or perhaps six required by average cargo vessels. Although there are a few exceptions, a sizable ship with more than one funnel may quite safely be put down as a

By courtesy of]   [Smith's Dock Co., Ltd.

A 120-FOOT TRAWLER

passenger liner. Each Company has its own distinguishing paint and a house flag which is generally flown when a ship is in port, and getting to know the different

[G. P. A.

PLEASURE STEAMER "CRESTED EAGLE" LEAVING LONDON BRIDGE FOR SOUTHEND AND MARGATE

colours and flags and the funnel markings is quite an interesting pursuit for anyone living in close contact with the docks or water front.

There are only a few *Paddle Steamers* left round the coast, and these are mostly used for daylight excursions, their advantage over the more economical screw steamers being that they have a huge deck for the accommodation of passengers and draw so little water that they can put in at any pier to land or embark. Although some

[Fox Photos.

A DRIFTER WITH ENGINE TROUBLE BEING TOWED INTO YARMOUTH HARBOUR

Hundreds of these drifters visit the North Sea fishing grounds in search of herrings.

223

of these ships are of eight or nine hundred tons they seldom require more than 8 or 9 feet of water.

In addition to these general types, there are all sorts of others that may sometimes be seen. Various authorities have fleets of their own ; the *Tenders* of Trinity House, for instance, which look after the lightships and carry the pilots, are well known, their hulls almost like those of yachts, and with smart paint and yellow funnels. Nearly every port has its *Dredgers*, some of them scooping the mud off the bottom by means of buckets running over a high ladder, others sucking it through a big tube.

Yachts may be of all sorts and types, and as many of them are converted fishing craft or merchantmen it is sometimes difficult to identify them except by their paint. According to custom, a yacht should be painted either white, or black with a white water-line ; this custom is more honoured in the breach than in observance ; the sails of some of the pleasure craft that knock about the coast in happy haphazard fashion are of anything but the snowy whiteness of tradition.

THE " RAGNA GORTHAN "
A typical Swedish timber ship.

[New York Times.

"CAMELS" USED IN THE WORK OF RAISING A LOST SUBMARINE
with their attendant tug, arriving at the scene of the disaster.

THE MARVELS OF SALVAGE

EVER since Man began to "go down to the sea in ships," salvage—which in its sea sense means the saving of sunken or wrecked ships, or their contents—has been practised in some form or other. Crude in its beginnings, wreck-recovery has now become an art, employing highly-skilled brains and costly plant.

Every country possessing a mercantile marine has salvage organizations of some kind. Perhaps the best known is the Liverpool and Glasgow Salvage Association, which operates all over the world's seas. Britain and America lead in salvage, with the Scandinavians close, while between the two wars the Italians carried out some striking salvage feats. During the war, our private companies, while retaining their identity, were taken over by the Admiralty and salvage became a matter of vital urgency. So pressing was our need for ships, that the salving of any vessel which it was considered could be subsequently repaired was worth while, regardless entirely of the cost involved. The salving of their war-material cargoes was equally important.

THE MARVELS OF SALVAGE

There was plenty of salvage to do. In normal times ships and cargoes to the value of millions yearly are wrecked from one cause or another. To such dangers as fog and storm must during wartime be added that arising from torpedoes, mines, and bombs. The greater the sea-risks the more demand for the salvor.

In peace time, the probable cost of salving a ship as well as the cost of later repairs have to be considered in comparison with the cost of building a new ship ; in other words, the salvage of a ship

[*Sport & General.*

MODEL SHOWING THE " LAURENTIC " AS SHE ORIGINALLY LAY, 120 FEET
BELOW THE SURFACE
Nearly the whole of the £5,000,000 worth of specie which went down in the ship has been recovered.

depends upon whether it is an economical proposition or not. A salvage officer will visit the wrecked ship and report on her condition and the probable extent of the damage. If she is worth salving he will instruct, say, the Liverpool and Glasgow Salvage Association or some other company. The Company sends its repair and other vessels to the scene of the wreck and sets about getting her afloat. Each job has to be tackled as circumstances suggest ; no fixed rules can be applied. Curious expedients are adopted sometimes. Upon one occasion a troopship that had sunk alongside a harbour pier was righted by hitching her to several railway engines and thus pulling her bodily upright. There was a similar case in Bombay some little time ago.

A diver goes down and inspects the wreck before any active measures are taken. A diver's dress consists of a heavy suit with a glass-fronted helmet as headpiece. Only the hands are left uncovered, so that the diver may be able to feel what he cannot see. Heavy weights on feet and shoulders sink him. Whilst below, air is pumped down a tube attached to the top of his helmet. In the helmet there

[New York Times.
DIVER PREPARES TO INSPECT "ELISHA THOMPSON," SUNK BY MINE IN NOUMEA HARBOUR

is a valve that can be regulated for pressure. Should necessity arise, the diver can close this valve and float himself to the surface. But he will do this only as an extreme measure ; it is dangerous for a diver to ascend too quickly, owing to his blood having become aerated whilst below. The diver communicates with the surface by signalling with the life-line tied round his waist. Sometimes a telephone is used, but most divers object to them, as they do not like, in their responsible and hazardous work, being interfered with from above. Working tools are sent down by a rope. No matter how apparently clear the water, a diver can see very little whilst working at any depth. A sort of sixth sense, born of long experience, enables him to perform his dangerous task. By crawling round and about he ascertains what damage has been sustained and where. By his report those who must decide the mode of salvage are guided.

Divers cannot descend to an unlimited depth in the ordinary rubber suit. If one went down too far, the pressure would crush the

[*Illustrations Bureau.*

PREPARING TO RIGHT A CAPSIZED VESSEL

life out of him. In August, 1948, during experiments on a diving suit for rescue work at great depths, a Royal Naval diver established a new world record dive of 535 feet. The former record of 440 feet was held by America. Even at 150 feet the diver will have a water pressure of nearly 145,000 lbs. upon his body. Diving bells will carry men deeper, and an American inventor has designed a submarine from which a man can walk on to the floor of the sea. In wreck-raising mobility on the part of the diver is essential, but few

SUBMERSIBLE MOTOR PUMPS AT WORK ON THE
BLOCKSHIP " IPHEGENIA "

The vessel was sunk on the Belgian coast in one of the most famous naval
operations.

efforts are now made to raise the wreck itself from any depth.

When the operating plan has been settled, the diver must go down again. Probably he will have to shift some of the cargo. If a patch is to be affixed, the diver must put it on. If there is any shoring up, cementing, or cutting away to be done, the diver must do it. A clever device now commonly used in salvage work enables a diver whilst working under water to use an electrical cutter in place of the former acetylene flame for cutting the plates of a vessel, and cameras and searchlights can also be used under water.

Among the more common ways of raising a ship are lifting her bodily, pumping her out, and filling her with compressed air.

[Illustrations Bureau.

PUMPING OUT THE " LUTINE "

This vessel, a captured French frigate, was wrecked off Terschelling Island, Holland, early in the nineteenth century, when conveying nearly half a million pounds in specie. A considerable part of the treasure has been recovered at various times. The photograph shows sand and water being pumped into large straining-tanks.

Lifting is done by lighters specially constructed for the purpose, or possibly by " camels," that is, huge flexible cylinders filled with compressed air, which are sunk and attached to the ship so that they lift her as they rise toward the surface. The lifting lighters are operated somewhat differently. Thin tanks filled with water, they are submerged until their decks are almost awash. Enormous hawsers passed round the wreck in figure of eight fashion are made fast to the lighters, and the tanks of the latter are pumped out. As their buoyancy increases the lighters pull up the wreck until she is clear of the bottom. Then the lighters are towed along with the wreck between them. With luck, she may be got into safety at one lift, or a series of lifts may be required. Always the lighters are sunk at low tide and the moving done at high tide or thereabouts.

[New Tork Times.
LOWERING A PONTOON OR CAMEL TO A SUNKEN VESSEL

Some of these lighters have a lifting capacity of two thousand tons. The heaviest weight ever raised by them at one pull was a collier of 2,750 tons. She was hauled to the surface in the Firth of Forth.

" Lifting " a sunken vessel sometimes amounts simply to passing hawsers round her and then dragging her up by main force.

Sometimes it is possible to patch up the hull and to pump a ship out. In other cases the decks are built up until they rise above the surface and thus form a dam over which water can be pumped until the vessel has enough buoyancy to float.

At other times the salvage engineer achieves his purpose by constructing a coffer dam around the damaged part. A coffer dam is like a huge box, or rather three sides of a box, built out from the vessel's side in such a way that it encloses the rent in her hull. The water is then pumped out of the dam, leaving it a dry space in which men can work unhampered by tide or weather, until temporary

[*New York Times.*

TUGS ON EITHER SIDE OF THE LIBERTY SHIP " HORACE BINNEY "
Many massive steel hawsers have been passed underneath her keel to keep her afloat.

repairs have been made that will enable the ship to be taken into dock.

" Camels " filled with air were employed in raising the cruiser *Gladiator*, sunk off Yarmouth, Isle of Wight. Sir F. Young adapted them, and with their aid accomplished what many experts regarded an an impossible task. Now they are a recognized part of salvage appliances. But vessels are frequently lifted by compressed air without the assistance of " camels." In such cases the hull, or a sufficient number of compartments within it, is made water-tight, only a vent being left. Powerful pumps in the salvage ship drive

Photographs by] [*A. H. Hawke, Helston.*

BAD CASES ON THE CORNISH COAST

compressed air down into the wreck, and the air forces out the water through the vent left for that purpose. As the wreck becomes air-filled she grows buoyant and rises to the surface. In a sense it is like a big air bubble coming to the top, and care must be taken that pressure is so graduated that it does not lift off the deck bodily, for, strong as this is, it was designed to withstand pressure from above, not from below. Were this to happen she would go down again like a stone, and the whole job would have to be started again. But salvage is replete with such uncertainties. One never knows

Photograph by]   [A. H. Hawke, Helston.
A BAD CASE ON THE CORNISH COAST

when a spell of bad weather will come, or something give out un-expectedly, and destroy the results of days or weeks of labour.

To float a wreck upon air it is not always necessary to patch her up. Sometimes enough pressure can be forced down to hold the water in check. Looking, at such a time, into the space thus formed, one sees a wall of green water held up only by the air driven against it. Were the force relaxed the "wall" would tumble down instantly.

A remarkable instance of salvage by compressed air was that of the *S.S Gothland*, many years ago. Ashore on rocks off the Scilly

Isles, her bottom was torn out for a length of 150 feet. The salvors simply forced air into her until she floated, and then brought her into Southampton under her own steam. All the way, as she moved, one could look through her bottom and see the water underneath.

The value of compressed air in salvage was demonstrated during the war in connection with oil-tankers. They were provided with an auxiliary Diesel air-compressor, from which air-lines were led along the decks to connect with each separate oil tank. In the event of under-water damage due to mine, torpedo, or stranding, the ship's personnel immediately pumped compressed air into the affected compartment and could sometimes thus keep their invaluable tanker afloat and bring her safely home.

A portable air-compressor is a most useful part of salvage equipment. In conjunction with it a small winch, called an "air-hoist" is often employed and provides a means of raising out of the diver's way jagged plates or other material which he may have cut adrift. An air-compressor will also make possible the use of a pneumatic-riveter—or "windy-hammer" as it is universally called—and may at other times be the driving force for circular and band-saws, which are often needed for cutting away timber.

A most useful recent invention is the Cox Bolt Gun. This device, not unlike a "windy-hammer" in appearance, is simply a gun which, by means of an explosive charge, fires a bolt.

SUBMERSIBLE MOTOR PUMPS THAT WORKED IN THE FLOODED HOLD OF A VESSEL FOR THREE MONTHS WITHOUT BEING TAKEN OUT

This wonderful invention works as well submerged as from the deck of a vessel. The value of the cargo in this case was over £3,000,000.

THE MARVELS OF SALVAGE

Suppose an under-water patch over a hole is required. The steel patch, with drill-holes around its edges, is lowered into position ; the diver then holds his Cox Bolt Gun fair against one of the drill-holes and fires. The sharp-pointed and especially ridged bolt embeds itself rigidly in the damaged plate of the ship, leaving its screw-head protruding through the drill-hole in the patch. When the required number of bolts have been fired into position nuts are screwed home, the patch made water-tight, and pumping out can begin.

[Humphrey Joel.

THE FAMOUS ROSTRUM AT LLOYD'S

Above it is the bell of the sunken treasure ship " Lutine " (see note at foot of photograph on page 229). The bell is rung when announcements of special importance are to be made.

The Cox Bolt Gun is also used to fire a bolt having a hole bored through its length so that air may be pumped through from outside—an operation which has more than once saved the lives of men imprisoned in stranded submarines.

Another kind of patch was used in the case of the *Frederick Bartholdi*, a 7,100-ton vessel which stranded off the coast of Skye on Christmas Day, 1943. Examination showed the salvors that, unevenly supported on rocks, she had sagged and that large fractures in her side and bottom plating had resulted. She had broken her back. Experience told them that rigid steel patches would be useless as, when pumping out began and the vessel regained buoyancy, she would also tend to reassume her original shape, distorting and displacing the patches. So they ingeniously fitted rubber patches instead. These simply bulged as the vessel re-formed, but continued to keep out the water. The ship was successfully refloated.

Hundreds of the ships that were lost during the ruthless U-boat campaign sank in such deep water that the cost of recovery would have been more than they were worth. But many were salved. One of the appliances used in this work was a wonderful electric submersible pump, the invention of a Scotch engineer. This can be lowered to great depths and will work there quite satisfactorily. In fact, a case is on record in which a vessel, having caught fire, lowered this pump overboard and filled her holds with water until the fire was extinguished. Then the pump was lowered into the holds and emptied them again. Among other items of salvage plant, too, are suction dredges that will move 5,000 tons of water or sand per hour.

One of the most remarkable series of salvage operations was undertaken in connection with the old *Laurentic*, a liner of nearly 15,000 tons, which was torpedoed during the First World War, about fifteen miles off the coast of Donegal.

The photograph on page 226 shows her as she originally lay, 120 feet below the surface. Later on she was crumpled up by a great storm, and from this twisted mass of steel divers of the Royal Navy in three years salved nearly £5,000,000 worth of bullion, including hundreds of thousands of pounds worth of shillings and florins. Every piece of the wreck had to be blown up to enable the divers to reach the treasure.

Even more remarkable was the salvage, by the Italian Sorima Company, of the gold which went down in the P. & O Liner *Egypt* when she was sunk off Ushant in 1922. In over 400 feet of water, with strong currents, it was regarded as quite impossible and the underwriters who had paid the insurance had no great hopes when they let the company try in return for about 60 per cent. of the gold that they recovered.

The Italians worked with the steel diving dress, or rather case, and specially-invented gear of a most ingenious description. The diver was lowered at the end of a steel wire and the salvage vessels on the surface had to be manœuvred to his telephoned instructions so that their gear was dropped in exactly the right spot. In this way, by infinite patience, they cut right down into the ship's specie room, three decks down, and after every possible disappointment and discouragement they recovered no less than £1,183,000 in gold.

With everything costing so much it is very seldom worth while nowadays to try to salve the ship unless the job is an easy one. But the salvors are as ingenious as ever in getting at the cargo.

BELGIAN MOTOR CARGO LINER " STAVELOT "

Note her clean lines and ship-shape appearance. She is capable of carrying 10,875 tons cargo deadweight.

By courtesy of] [*Fairfield Shipbuilding Co., Ltd.*

CABLE STEAMER " LADY DENISON PENDER " (2,000 TONS), BELONGING TO CABLE & WIRELESS, LTD.

THE "SAN FELIX"

A good example of the modern oil "Tanker." The engines are placed as far aft as possible to reduce the danger of fire with a cargo so inflammable.

A TYPICAL BRITISH COLLIER BEING LOADED

Photo]   [*H. Jenkins, Lowestoft.*

SCENE ABOARD A DEEP-SEA TRAWLER

THE HARVEST OF THE SEA

THE STORY OF THE FISHING FLEET

IF you are on a big liner or cross-channel ship approaching the shore of new country or even returning to one of your home ports, you will, at some distance from your destination, pass ships with black hulls, smoking funnels and two masts, the aftmost of which has a tiny triangular sail. These ships are together in twos or threes and invariably wallow heavily in the sea. If you are fortunate enough to pass close, you may see them at work. They will be trawlers or drifters garnering the harvest of the sea. They are among the most hard-worked and picturesque of all the many ship types. Their crews are among the hardiest and must suffer many privations in getting a hard-earned living from watery depths.

There is a certain basic similarity between all kinds of fishing craft which leads the uninitiated to dub them trawlers. This is not actually true, however, because there are considerable differences between the various types, excluding for the moment the little off-shore fishing ships which are mostly open boats manned by local

239

fishermen, who, incidentally, form the basis of our life-boat crews. Fishing craft, generally speaking, fall under four heads, according to the work which they carry out : (1) *trawling*, (2) *drifting*, (3) *line fishing* and (4) *seine netting*. The first, as far as Great Britain at any rate is concerned, is easily the most important, and in its earliest form, according to Mr. H. N. Binns, a well-known authority on the subject, was carried out by sailing smacks of between 60 and 90 feet in length which dragged along the bed a bag-shaped net, having its mouth held open by two vertical iron frames supporting a horizontal wooden beam attached to the vessel by a single manila warp or rope. The type still survives to a small extent at Lowestoft on the East Coast and comprises many picturesque craft, which with their brown sails make a beautiful picture. Towards the end of the nineteenth century, steel-hulled vessels with steam engines began to appear and the beam gear, as it was called, gave place to what is now known as the ottertrawl, which, with improvements, is still used to-day. This comprises, roughly speaking, a bag-shaped net narrowed off at the aft or rear end and having a piece bitten out of the forward end in both the upper and lower sheet. The mouth of the net is kept open in the horizontal sense by two spreaders or trawl boards, each attached

Photo]   [*H. Jenkins, Lowestoft.*

ON THE DECK OF A NORTH SEA TRAWLER

Photo]   [*H. Jenkins, Lowestoft.*

HAULING IN THE HERRING NETS AT SUNRISE

to the towing vessel by a steel wire rope. These wires are shackled to brackets on the forward part of the doors and thus, as the ship goes ahead, the boards spread as far apart as the net between them allows. It is interesting to remember that trawls vary in size from 60 feet on the headline in the case of a smaller ship to 130 feet in the case of a large vessel fishing on smooth ground, the usual sizes being from 80 to 100 feet from wing end to wing end and about 120 feet in overall length. There are many types of trawlers, the smaller ones usually operating in the North Sea and Irish Sea, whilst middle-size ones between 110 and 135 feet, fish the outer waters of the North Sea and the Faroe Islands from Aberdeen and the Humber ports, off the west coast of Scotland, from Fleetwood ; and off the south of Ireland from the Welsh ports of Milford Haven, Swansea and Cardiff. Then there are the large boats of up to 180 feet in length which go to Iceland, Bear Island, the White Sea, Greenland and the Davis Straits and which come steaming home with full cargoes of fish, literally covered in ice. Some of the largest and most modern trawlers are fitted with refrigerated compartments, and are equipped with all modern navigational aids. Such vessels may cost anything up to £100,000 apiece.

Photo]   *[H. Jenkins, Lowestoft.*

HAULING IN THE TRAWL NETS

Drifting is carried out with a special type of vessel, quite different from the trawler. The drifter does not tow a net but literally lays a wall of netting in the upper waters and rides to it, the size of the mesh being such that a herring or mackerel can get its head and gills through but not its whole body. The drifters shoot anything up to one hundred nets, each one in fishing order being 40 yards long and 40 feet deep approximately. Thus, according to Mr. Binns, " a wall of netting over two miles long is laid " ! Drifter fishing, that of the East Coast, starts off the Shetlands in the spring and year after year the fish are caught in the same spot and in the same week as they come down the East Coast. It reaches its height in the Home Fishing off Yarmouth in October and November, when hundreds of drifters are to be found working from the ports of Yarmouth and Lowestoft and which, when all in port together, literally block the whole river. Drift nets are made of strong cotton twine and are frequently treated with special preservative known as cutch. Usually a drift net will last for a number of years, but if a vessel should lose its whole fleet of nets as it is called, the cost of replacement may be over £1,000. Drifters are usually from 50 to 100 feet in length and are similar in hull form to a trawler. They are invariably distinguishable at sea because their fore-mast is usually lowered on to the top of their deck house and they have a mainsail spread on their mizzen mast aft.

Line fishing is an important branch of the fishing industry and is carried out by ships of all sizes, from a small off-shore boat to power-driven vessels of upwards of 130 feet in length. The method is the same in all cases, namely by means of a main line with branches from it, each bearing a baited hook. A typical ship running from Aberdeen for example, will shoot as many as 30 baskets of lines each containing 480 fathoms of main line with a branch line and hook every 3 fathoms, a total of 15 miles of line and over 5,000 hooks. Naturally, there is a tremendous amount of work to do in handling gear of this size even when mechanical methods are employed since the fish have to be taken off every hook individually and the hook is then examined and coiled down ready to be put into the water again.

Seine netting is not much used in this country, although it is becoming increasingly popular. Actually, it is of Scandinavian origin and a net similar in general form to an otter-trawl mentioned above is used. It is larger, however, and made of light twine and mounted on light rope. The vessel drops a buoy to which an end of a manila warp or rope is attached. She then steams out carrying this warp. Having paid out almost 1,000 fathoms, she turns virtually at right

Photo]   *[H. Jenkins, Lowestoft.*

LANDING THE CATCH

angles and pays out the nets. Then another turn brings her head towards the starting-point, and she pays out the second warp. Arriving back at the buoy, the first warp is taken on board and by hauling on both warps the net is dragged gently towards the vessel.

These are the main ways in which fish is caught in British waters, and what has been said applies in general to the waters of other countries, too. There are also special methods of dory fishing ; i.e. fishing from a small boat attached to a large vessel in American waters, whilst the Spanish employ two drifter-sized vessels towing a large, light net between them. These are known as pair or " Pareja " fishing ships. In each case, the craft under consideration is of steel or wood construction, although the latter is becoming less popular and all vessels, whether small off-shore boats or large ocean-going craft, have some form of power. Many of the larger ships employ steam because this is useful, for example, for processing the livers of cod, heating the vessel and thawing the nets in Arctic waters ; but the majority of smaller ships now employ internal combustion engines, either petrol or of the diesel type. These remarks apply too, to ships of long-distance type fishing the Newfoundland Coast Banks. The fishing industry is one of the most important of all our national businesses and employs thousands of men and women.

Photo]   [*H. Jenkins, Lowestoft.*

A HERRING DRIFTER IN HEAVY SEAS

Photo]   [*Marconi's Wireless Telegraph Co., Ltd.*

THE LIGHTHOUSE AT START POINT

Fitted with a Marconi wireless beacon transmitter operating on a wave-length of 100 metres.

WIRELESS AT SEA

THE introduction of wireless telegraphy at the beginning of the century made a great difference to shipping in many ways, though it is principally thought of in connection with the saving of life. To many, in spite of the development of broadcasting, wireless is still an unexplained mystery. In principle, it is very simple. One has only to think of a calm pond into which a stone is thrown, causing the ripples to extend outward in all directions. It is the same with wireless, but of course the waves cannot be seen, and instead of a single stone disturbing the water, the atmosphere is disturbed by electric " waves " that can be detected and amplified by properly sensitive instruments in the distance.

After the first early experiments by Marconi and others, the distances over which messages could be sent were constantly increased. The first occasion on which wireless proved its possibilities for saving life and property at sea was in 1899, when a steamer named the *F.F. Matthews* ran into the East Goodwin lightship, damaging her severely. The station on the South Foreland received a wireless call for help, and steamers were immediately sent from Dover.

In 1900 a message was sent from the Lizard, in Cornwall, to the

Isle of Man. This was followed soon afterwards by messages right across the Atlantic to Newfoundland. It was then discovered that much greater distances could be covered at night than by daylight. The Cunard Company was one of the first British lines to take up wireless enthusiastically : as early as 1904 the *Campania* published a daily newspaper on board with news received by wireless. The news service proved a great boon to passengers, who were otherwise completely cut off from shore, and it is now an everyday feature of an ocean voyage. Notwithstanding this progress, there were still many who scoffed at wireless as unreliable and uncertain, but at the beginning of 1909 an accident occurred which converted everybody.

The White Star liner *Republic*, with a large number of passengers on board, was, early one morning, rammed and sunk some 175 miles from the Ambrose light off New York by the Italian emigrant ship *Florida*. Both ships were in a bad way, and the crowd of emigrants on board the Italian got into a state of panic and prevented full measures being taken for saving life. The wireless operator of the *Republic*, a youngster named Jack Binns, stuck to his instrument hour after hour, sending out the " C.Q.D.," the distress signal used before the S.O.S. was introduced for simplicity. As a result help was speedily sent, and though it was not possible to get the ship to port, only two lives were lost. This incident caused a great interest to be taken in wireless telegraphy, and Operator Binns was feted somewhat hysterically as a hero all over the country, though he himself described his action as " merely doing his job." Shortly afterwards wireless became almost universal for steamers of any size.

By courtesy of] [*Marconi's Wireless Telegraph Co., Ltd.*
A WIRELESS SET FOR USE IN LIFE-BOATS
The transmitter is worked by power generated by the main motor.

WIRELESS AT SEA

When the 1914-18 war broke out further great progress had been made. For instance, a simple invention known as a Wireless Direction Finder had been introduced, enabling the direction of wireless messages to be accurately determined. Thus it became possible for a would-be rescuing ship to steer direct for a ship sending out distress calls even though she could not give her position. Unfortunately, this also meant that submarines could readily locate merchant ships which used wireless—and for this reason the Admiralty during the last war imposed strict " wireless silence " on merchant ships. At the same time wireless enabled the Admiralty to move whole fleets as easily as a chess-player moves his pieces, and was responsible for saving thousands of lives from ships that had been attacked.

Considering its recent introduction it is wonderful to what diverse uses wireless is put nowadays. First of all, there is the fact that a colossal number of messages are sent both

THE WIRELESS ROOM IN A LINER

to and from ships and between shore stations. A great ship like the *Queen Mary* could not possibly find time in twenty-four hours to send or receive all her messages, and therefore runs several wireless stations on different wave-lengths. In addition, high-speed sending and receiving gear is fitted, so that several words a second can be dealt with and time saved. Not only does a modern ship use her wireless for distress signals, but also for business purposes, telling her owners just when she is likely to arrive, so that everything may be ready for her and expensive and vexatious delay avoided. Similarly she receives instructions from her owners, and is frequently diverted to other ports. Passengers can make all their arrangements for taxis and hotel accommodation while still at sea and warn their friends of their arrival. The officers of the ship receive time signals sent out by Rugby Radio and several other stations throughout the world for checking the accuracy of their chronometers.

Perhaps the most important development of wireless, however, is that of navigation by RADAR, which letters stand for Radio Direction and Range. We all know that if we stand near a cliff and shout loudly an echo comes back. This is a sound echo, the waves of which travel at 1,100 feet per second. The principle of radar is that radio waves, travelling at the enormous speed of 186,000 miles per second, will strike any surface object within range and be reflected back to the ship's instrument as a radio echo. Land, other ships, icebergs, harbour buoys and beacons are objects thus detected and illuminated on a special screen. Simultaneously, their distance and bearing are measured. The value of radar in dense fog becomes obvious—the ship's navigator, who would otherwise be " blind ", can now " see " the dangers ahead of him.

By courtesy of]   [Marconi's Wireless Telegraph Co., Ltd.

FLYING BRIDGE OF THE S.S. " EMPRESS OF CANADA "

On the left are the fixed frames of the direction-finder, with the range-finder and standard compass in the centre, and the steering wheels on the right.

RADIO ROOM IN THE " QUEEN MARY "

The last war also saw the development of other means of navigation by wireless. There are the Decca Navigator, Loran, and Consol systems, by means of which a ship can fix her position with a remarkable degree of accuracy. The Decca Navigator was used on D-Day with great success by leading ships of that gigantic seaborne invasion of the Normandy beaches. The instrument in the ship receives its power by radio transmission from certain land stations, and when the readings on the dials are plotted on special charts the ship's position is " fixed."

Normally, a tramp steamer has no need to keep a constant wireless watch as does a crack Atlantic liner, yet she may be just as useful for saving lives from a sinking ship. An ingenious invention, therefore, rings an alarm bell when a distress call is received.

Similarly, for coasters, fishing vessels and the like, an inexpensive and simple, but reliable, system of wireless telephony is on the market, and radio enthusiasts who wander off the wave-lengths of the broadcasting stations will often get a shock to find themselves listening to trawler skippers exchanging their own private views and news on the fishing grounds.

By courtesy of] [A. & J. Inglis, Ltd.
" PENLEE " No. 5 TRINITY HOUSE PILOT CUTTER

THE PILOT AND HIS DUTIES

"WE'RE picking up the pilot!" In tramp or liner, this is always thrilling news and no man is watched with greater interest than the pilot who boards a homecoming ship. But if the voyage is nearly over, intricate waters lie ahead and the pilot's duties are only beginning. His task is no small one, and a complete knowledge of local conditions must be combined with the ability to handle ships with a sure and ready touch. Shoal waters, narrow passages and the traffic of other ships frequently call for magnificent seamanship.

Different districts and ports have different governing bodies, but one of the most notable pilot services is that of The Corporation of the Trinity House of Deptford, Stroud, covering the approaches to London, Southampton, and a number of smaller ports. The pilots on this service are liner officers who have left the sea with the highest qualifications and settled down in one of the most comfortable, although one of the most responsible, billets that the sea has to offer. Landsmen sometimes mistakenly suppose that when a pilot is on the bridge the responsibility of the captain ceases. This is not so. The captain is at all times responsible to his owners for the safety of their vessel and, theoretically, the pilot acts in the capacity of an expert adviser on local navigation. In practice, however, the pilot gives the orders and a captain intervenes only in emergency.

It will be asked how Trinity House pilots get their jobs and what qualifications they must possess. For one thing they must be Master Mariners and must have been at least seven years at sea with an absolutely clean record. Until recently it was necessary to have served for a year as an officer of a sailing ship, but there are so few of such vessels left that this rule had to be relaxed. He must, at his own expense, spend many weeks going up and down the waters which his licence will cover.

If a ship's officer has all these qualifications, and can satisfy the authorities that he is a fit and proper man for the position, they will put his name down and will let him know when there is a vacancy in the service. Vacancies are scarce and the list of applicants is long, so that when the summons comes he must be prepared to respond to it at once or the opportunity may not occur again. For three years after he has been enrolled the pilot will not be allowed to take charge of any ship drawing more than fourteen feet of water, and at the end of that time he has to pass a very stiff examination before he is promoted. Once he has got his step he may be called upon, while still a young man, to take the biggest ship in the world into port at short notice, and this is a rather terrifying experience. Most of the big companies, however, have their " choice " pilots who always look after their ships and have often belonged to the Line previously.

Assuming that a ship is coming up to London, she may have put in to one of the Channel ports to pick up the " choice " pilot of her Company, but if not she must stop and take one on board at Dungeness or off Harwich. If her captain tried to take her up without help he would, except in certain circumstances, be fined.

When the pilot cutter sees an approaching vessel flying the International Code flag " G "—which means, " I require a pilot," she manœuvres into a suitable position and the next man on the roll for duty is transferred to the ship by small boat—no easy matter in sometimes troubled waters. The deck of the ship is gained by means of a rope ladder hanging overside, and as soon as he is on board the pilot goes up to the bridge, which will probably be in the charge of the captain, and indicates what course to steer. The captain may have been up the River many hundreds of times before, but all sorts of things may have happened to the channel since the last occasion, and the pilot must be right up-to-date in every particular. An obstruction may not have been in the fairway longer than an hour or two, but he has to know all about it. Dredging may be in operation ; divers may be at work somewhere ; a buoy may be temporarily out of position, or a certain dock closed. A captain could not possibly be aware of all such local changes and it is for this reason that the employment of a pilot is compulsory in many areas. At Gravesend the Dungeness pilot lands and another pilot comes on board who specializes in the River, and at the entrance of the dock to which a ship is bound yet another pilot, this time a waterman, takes charge.

The authorities arrange that the pilots shall be paid according to the draught of the ship they are handling, as there is obviously more chance of a deep ship going ashore than of a shallow one doing so. Some allowance is, however, made for size. In order to make everything quite fair, the pilots themselves generally arrange to pool their fees, so that nobody has to suffer by having to handle the first ship that comes along.

Whenever a ship is in charge of a duly-certificated pilot she flies —generally between her masts—a red and white flag, divided vertically (see letter H in colour plate).

THE " BEAVERLAKE," C.P.S., DOCKING AT MONTREAL

THE " QUEEN MARY " IN THE KING GEORGE V GRAVING DOCK AT
SOUTHAMPTON

CHINESE JUNKS REEFED DOWN IN A BREEZE

SEA TERMS AND THEIR MEANING

IN reading stories of the sea or books of travel you will often come across words or expressions that are rarely used except at sea. Every sailor knows their meaning, and many landsmen pretend to, but are hopelessly wrong. If you read and remember the following notes, you will know more than a great many people. Other sea terms are explained in the various articles on sailing ships and liners.

A 1. Classed by Lloyd's Register as in first-class condition.

A.B. Able-bodied ; higher and more experienced than an " ordinary seaman."

Abaft. Behind, or on the side near the stern, as " abaft the deck-house."

Aft. Near the stern, or behind the vessel.

Athwart or *thwart.* Across, generally across the ship ; as the thwarts or seats on which rowers sit.

Ballast. Heavy material, such as iron, lead, bags of sand or shot, barrels or tanks of water, carried in the bottom of a ship to steady her or prevent her leaning over too easily when the wind blows against her side or sails.

Battens. Strips of wood or flat iron bars used to fasten down the tarpaulins covering hatches.

Beat. To sail with the wind first on one bow and then the other.

Before. In front of ; as before the deck-house ; on the side nearer the bows.

Belay. To fasten a rope round a cleat or belaying pin.

Belaying pins. Large bolts round which the ropes are twisted to fasten them.

Bell. The ship's bell is rung in a certain way at sea to indicate the time, every half-hour. At noon, by observation, eight strokes are given in four pairs of strokes ; at 12.30, one stroke ; at one o'clock, two strokes ; at 1.30 two strokes and after a short pause a third stroke ; at two o'clock, two pairs of strokes, and so on to four o'clock when four pairs of strokes, or " eight bells," are sounded. From four o'clock to six o'clock and from six o'clock to eight o'clock are the first and second " dog watches," and in these the greatest number of strokes, until eight bells, is four bells ; but after that the bells are rung in the usual way until the following noon.

Berth. A sleeping place ; the place where a ship lies.

Bilge. The curved part of a ship where the sides and bottom meet.

Bilge keel. A keel or projection fastened to the outside of the curve, for about two-thirds of the vessel's length, to reduce rolling.

Binnacle. The stand for the compass by which the vessel is steered.

Boom. A spar extending from a mast to stretch or extend a sail.

Bows. The two sides at the front of a vessel ; that on the right is the starboard bow, that on the left the port bow.

Bowsprit. A spar projecting in front of the bows, and secured in place by various ropes, those to each side being " shrouds," and those beneath " bobstays."

Bridge. A light structure extending across a steamer ; reserved for the captain and other navigating officers.

Bulkhead. A wall or partition in the interior of a vessel.

Bulwarks. The raised sides round a vessel's deck.

Bunk. A fixed sleeping berth.

SEA TERMS AND THEIR MEANING

Buoy. A floating iron can moored by a chain on the edge of a shoal to mark a safe channel ; buoys are of a great variety of shapes, all of which have a definite meaning to the sailor ; some carry bells rung by the motion of the sea, and others gas lamps which burn night and day for weeks at a time.

Caboose. The cook's galley in small vessels or sailing ships, on the deck forward.

Capstan. A revolving post fastened to the deck to haul up an anchor ; worked by steam or by men at the capstan bars.

Charthouse. A small deck-house in which the charts are kept ; adjoins the bridge and is sometimes next the captain's cabin.

" *Chips.*" Nickname for ship's carpenter.

Close-hauled. Sailing close to the wind.

Companion. A staircase or ladder leading from the deck to an apartment below ; also the hatch-covering over this.

Crow's Nest. A barrel-shaped look-out place on the foremast ; usually accommodates two men.

Cuddy. A small cabin ; a cooking galley.

Cutter. A one-masted fore-and-aft rigged sailing vessel or a naval pulling boat.

Davits. Steel or iron cranes, usually fitted in pairs at the sides of a ship for raising and lowering boats from and to the water.

"*Davy Jones's Locker.*" The bottom of the sea.

Dead Reckoning. An estimate of the ship's position by the distance travelled, as shown by the log, etc., is called " dead reckoning." Thought by some to have been originally *deduced reckoning.* This is checked whenever possible by observation of the sun and stars.

Deadlights. Wood or metal coverings over portholes or windows ; used in bad weather to prevent the sea smashing the glass.

Derelict. A forsaken ship.

Dinghy. A small open boat.

"*Doctor.*" Nickname for a ship's cook.

Easting. The degrees of longitude when sailing eastward.

Fathom. Six feet. Lead lines always, and charts showing depth of water generally, are marked in fathoms.

Fender. A long wooden beam usually swinging at the side of a pier or dock to prevent ships chafing against it. Globular-shaped plaited rope, or pudding fenders, are generally used when a vessel is moving alongside another or a landing-stage to lessen the shock of contact.

Flotsam. Goods thrown into the sea from a ship and still afloat.

Fore, or Forward. Opposite to " aft." The fore or front part of a vessel.

Forecastle. A small raised deck forward ; also the accommodation for the crew beneath this deck.

Foul. Dirty, tangled.

Freeboard. The vessel's side above water amidships.

Gunwale. The top of the sides of a boat.

Half deck. A half-decked boat is one only partly decked. The apprentices' quarters in the old sailing ships.

Halliard. A rope or chain for raising or lowering a sail or flag.

Hatch. An opening in a deck for passengers or cargo, one with a sliding top is a " booby-hatch."

Hawse-pipes. Holes in the bows, or occasionally the stern, through which the anchor chains are passed.

Heel. To lean over to one side.

Helm. The tiller or handle controlling the rudder.

Hold. The interior of a ship for cargo.

Hurricane Deck. The topmost deck in a large steamship.

Jetsam. Goods thrown overboard and washed ashore.

Jettison. To throw cargo or heavy gear overboard in order to lighten the vessel.

Jigger Mast. The fourth mast in a vessel.

Jury. Temporary make-shift, as a jury mast.

Ketch. A vessel with one large mast and the after mast small ; there are many varieties of this rig.

Knot. See nautical mile.

Lee. The side of a vessel opposite to that against which the wind is blowing.

Lee Shore. Shore on the lee side of a ship.

Leeway. The sideways movement of a vessel when the wind is blowing on her side.

Leeboards. Large boards lowered on the weather sides of flat-bottomed vessels to prevent them making so much leeway.

List. To lean to one side.

Load line. The depths to which a ship may be loaded, indicated by a white circle with a white line through it, painted on the outside of every ship, called the Plimsoll mark.

Log. An instrument towed astern to measure and record the speed at which a vessel is travelling through the water. The ship's diary.

" *Mother Cary's Chickens.*" Stormy petrels ; a small gull about the size of a pigeon.

Nautical Mile, or *Knot.* A sixtieth of a degree of latitude at the Equator. A knot is the same distance when estimating the speed of a vessel per hour, thus a speed of ten knots means ten

SEA TERMS AND THEIR MEANING

knots an hour ; a knot is never a measure of distance only ; 60 nautical miles equal 69½ geographical miles.

Painter. A rope fastened in the bows of a small boat to fasten it to another. To cut the painter ; to cut the rope to get away in a hurry.

Poop. A raised deck at the after end of a vessel. A vessel is said to be " pooped " when a wave washes over her from the stern.

Port. The left-hand side of a vessel ; the circular windows in the side of a ship or deck-house.

Quarter. The side of a vessel near the stern.

Raking. Sloping—masts not upright are said to rake.

Ratlines. Small ropes fastened to the shrouds to enable the sailors to go aloft.

Reef. To reduce a sail by tying a part of it by small ropes called reef points.

Scuppers. Openings in the ship's bulwarks to let off the sea water which may come on board.

Scuttle. To sink a ship by cutting a hole in her or opening sea cocks. A port hole.

Shrouds. Steel wire ropes extending from the mast to the sides of the ship to hold the masts steady.

Stanchions. Wooden or steel uprights supporting a deck or handrail.

Starboard. The right-hand side of a vessel.

Stays. Ropes supporting a mast and leading in the direction of the length of vessel.

Syren. A fog-horn operated by compressed air or steam.

Tack. To change the direction when sailing to windward. A vessel with the wind on the starboard side is on the starboard tack ; and with the wind on the port side is on the port tack.

Watch. See under " Bells." On duty. A division of the ship's crew.

Weather. The side of a vessel against which the wind is blowing.

FINNISH STEEL FOUR-MASTED BARQUE